Beyond Alternations

STANFORD MONOGRAPHS IN LINGUISTICS

The aim of this series is to make exploratory work
that employs new linguistic data, extending the scope or domain
of current theoretical proposals, available to a wide audience.
These monographs will provide an insightful generalization
of the problem and data in question which will be
of interest to people working in a variety of frameworks.

STANFORD MONOGRAPHS IN LINGUISTICS

BEYOND ALTERNATIONS

A Constructional Model of the German Applicative Pattern

Laura A. Michaelis
&
Josef Ruppenhofer

CSLI
PUBLICATIONS
Center for the Study of
Language and Information
Stanford, California

Center for the Study of Language and Information
Leland Stanford Junior University
Printed in the United States
05 04 03 02 01   5 4 3 2 1

Library of Congress Cataloging-in-Publication Data

Michaelis, Laura A., 1964–
Beyond alternations : a constructional model of the German applicative pattern / Laura Michaelis, Josef Ruppenhofer.
p. cm.
Includes bibliographical references and index.

ISBN 1-57586-329-4 (cloth : alk. paper)
ISBN 1-57586-330-8 (paper : alk. paper)

1. Grammar, Comparative and general—Verb phrase.
2. Grammar, Comparative and general—Syntax.
3. Semantics.
I. Ruppenhofer, Josef, 1971– . II. Title.
P281.M54 2001
415 2001037828
CIP

The drawing, "Développement du Va-et-Vient du Devidage," that appears on the cover of the paperback edition of this book is from the *Encyclopédie ou Dictionnaire Raisonneé des Sciences des Arts et des Métiers*, edited by Diderot. Première Édition de 1751–1780.

∞ The acid-free paper used in this book meets the minimum requirements of the American National Standard for Information Sciences—Permanence of Paper for Printed Library Materials, ANSI Z39.48-1984.

CSLI was founded early in 1983 by researchers from Stanford University, SRI International, and Xerox PARC to further research and development of integrated theories of language, information, and computation. CSLI headquarters and CSLI Publications are located on the campus of Stanford University.

CSLI Publications reports new developments in the study of language, information, and computation. In addition to lecture notes, our publications include monographs, working papers, revised dissertations, and conference proceedings. Our aim is to make new results, ideas, and approaches available as quickly as possible. Please visit our web site at

http://cslipublications.stanford.edu/

for comments on this and other titles, as well as for changes and corrections by the author and publisher.

In memory of our fathers,
Leon A. Michaelis (1915-1997) and
Joseph Ruppenhofer (1932-1999)

Contents

Acknowledgments

Among the various linguists whose work and constructive criticism have enriched and informed the present monograph, we would like to single out former and current members of the Berkeley linguistics community, including in particular Charles Fillmore, Paul Kay, Adele Goldberg and George Lakoff. We gratefully acknowledge Michael Knölker, Marianne Ruppenhofer and Christian Fleischmann for their patient and insightful assistance with the German data. Our thanks also go to Nurit Melnik for her generous editorial help. We are also grateful to the International Computer Science Institute in Berkeley for supporting our research activities and to Bill Raymond, Michelle Gregory, Anne Timberlake and Ramona Michaelis for facilitating our interstate travel. We also thank an anonymous reviewer for helpful comments on an earlier version of this monograph. Finally, we would like to express our gratitude to Dikran Karaguezian, Kim Lewis Brown, and Chris Sosa at CSLI for their editorial and moral support during the preparation of this monograph.

1 Introduction

Compositional theories of sentence semantics have been centrally concerned with the relationship between the meanings of lexical items and the meanings of sentences which contain those lexical items. Verbal argument structure has been of great interest in recent theory building because of the transparent nature of the relationship between the verb's semantic requirements and the number and kind of thematic roles in the sentence. The majority of theories of verbal argument structure accord a central place to the concept of ALTERNATION, exploring the nature of the relationship between argument frames licensed by a given verb. The recognition that argument-structure alternations are licensed by narrow semantic classes of verbs (Levin 1993, Gropen et al. 1989) has led to lexically-based accounts of alternations, most of which posit minimally specified verbal valence structures along with general principles ('linking rules') governing the interface between verbal thematic structure and surface syntax.

While the general principles are typically based upon some version of Fillmore's (1986) semantic-role hierarchy, the greatest attention has been paid to those cases in which linkings to the core grammatical functions do not follow the predictions of the hierarchy. Mappings of this type are described by two general approaches. In the first approach, semantic (e.g., Aktionsart) representation is held constant, and the marked patterns are viewed as violations of mapping constraints (Foley and Van Valin 1984) . The existence of the marked patterns may be attributed to optimization elsewhere in the system, including the achievement of a match between a given thematic role and a given functional role (e.g., location and topic in Bresnan's (1994) analysis of locative inversion). In the second approach, the mapping constraints are assumed to be inviolable, while the lexico-semantic representations which provide inputs to those rules are manipulated through semantic operations on decomposed lexical structure (Gropen et al. 1989, Wunderlich 1997).

Each model has been applied to the problem of the locative alternation. In the marked member of this alternation, a goal or location argument, which would otherwise receive oblique coding, receives the coding prototypically associated with patienthood (Foley and Van Valin 1984, Dowty 1991, Van Valin and Lapolla 1997). This pattern, exemplified by the English sentence *She smeared the canvas with paint*, has been viewed as theoretically important because its interpretation, involving an attribution of 'affectedness' to the goal argument, suggests something noncompositional about the operation of the lexical rule. Is this lexical rule adding meaning? The facts of German, while superficially similar to those of English, force us to address an additional, more fundamental question: Is there a lexical rule at all?

At first glance, the locative alternation recognized for English and other languages finds a straightforward parallel in German, with two obvious differences. First, the oblique-promoting device in German, like Bantu applicatives (Alsina and Mchombo 1990, Wunderlich 1991), involves morphological marking on the verb—in the case of German, the inseparable prefix *be-*. Thus, for example, the applicative counterpart of the German verb *schmieren* 'smear' is *beschmieren*, as in *Sie beschmierte die Leinwand mit Farbe* 'She smeared the canvas with paint'. Second, the German applicative linking pattern combines with both intransitive and transitive verbs. That is, it accepts both transitive verbs denoting transfer, like *schmieren*, and bivalent intransitives denoting location or locomotion, e.g., *wandern* 'wander'. This verb alternates with bivalent transitive *bewandern*, as in *Sie bewanderte den Schwarzwald* 'She wandered the Black Forest'. In each case, the location argument, which would otherwise receive oblique (preposition phrase) coding, is expressed by a direct grammatical function (a direct object in the case of active voice). In the latter case, the applicative has a TRANSITIVIZING function. As a number of theorists, including Marcus et al. (1995) and Brinkmann (1997), have observed, the German applicative is both productive and constrained: a great many verbs have applicative alternates and yet these verbs appear to cluster into relatively narrow semantic classes. In this regard, of course, the German applicative behaves much like its English analog, as described by Pinker (1989) and Levin (1993), *inter alia*. For example, causative verbs of position like English *lean* (or German *lehnen*) do not generally form acceptable applicative sentences, as in **She leaned the field with ladders*.

Nothing that we have said thus far is inconsistent with a model of the German applicative pattern in which a lexical rule mediates between two entries for a given verb. This general type of model works whether the alternates are bivalent or trivalent and whether or not the two verb entries related by the rule are assumed to contain identical sets of semantic entailments. However, a more comprehensive look at the inventory of verbs which license the applicative pattern in German suggests that we need a broader conception of the function of this pattern than that suggested by a lexical-rule based approach. This broader picture includes examples which cannot be reconciled with the general claim that the German applicative is a device for 'promoting' location arguments that would otherwise receive oblique coding. In certain of these examples, illustrated in (1.1), the 'input' lexical entry is (arguably) trivalent but does not license a goal argument:[1]

(1.1) Message ID <6lXJdRgaxSB@p-klink.link-dd.CL.sub.de>
Aber wenn ich es mir recht überlege habe ich mich von meinen Kollegen [...] auch mal eifrig mit Kaffee **bekochen** lassen [...]
'But, if I remember correctly, at times I also let myself be *be*-cooked with coffee by my colleagues [...]'

In (1.1), *be*-prefixation has an effect similar to that of the English ditransitive pattern in allowing the linking of a BENEFICIARY to a core grammatical function (cf. *He made them coffee*). The base verb in (1.1), *kochen* 'cook', does not license an oblique expression denoting a goal, as illustrated by the ill-formed permutation **Ich habe meine Kollegen Kaffee zu mir kochen lassen*, whose English translation is the equally ill-formed **I had my colleagues make coffee to me.* In certain bivalent applicative examples, exemplified in (1.2), the base verb could conceivably be said to select for a location argument, but assigns this argument direct rather than oblique coding:

(1.2) Message ID: <37ba6d95@news.dvs.org>
Es reicht Selzer, hier andere aufrichtige Leute als Neonazis zu **beschimpfen** und anderweitig zu verleumden geht zu weit [...]
'That's enough, Selzer! Verbally abusing (lit. *be*-scolding) other decent people by calling them Neo-Nazis and slandering them in other ways goes too far [...].'

[1]Our data come from six different sources and are identifiable in the following ways: data from the on-line corpora at the *Institut für deutsche Sprache* start out with a sequence of capital letters and numbers coding the specific corpus they are taken from e.g. WK=Wendekorpus); data from the Deja Usenet Archive at the Google website start out with 'Message Id'; data from the Lexis-Nexis research service start out with the name of the journal, newspaper, or magazine the quote is taken from e.g. *Süddeutsche Zeitung*); data from the *Frankfurter Rundschau Korpus* are marked by a single number. Data from websites are given in the standard URL format. Examples which were provided by native-speaker consultants carry no marking.

In (1.2), the bivalent base verb *schimpfen* 'scold' is transitive rather than intransitive;[2] the 'location' argument (the recipient) receives direct-object coding in both applicative and nonapplicative alternates. The relationship between *schimpfen* and *beschimpfen* is therefore not analogous to that which holds between other bivalent verbs, like *wandern* 'wander' and *bewandern*: *be*-prefixation in (1.2) does not transitivize. Another problematic class of bivalent applicative verbs are those whose base verb is monovalent. This class is exemplified in (1.3) for the verb *lügen* 'lie':

(1.3) Message ID <37CCFA53.12B18AA2@t-online.de>
Die Teilnehmer an dieser Studie haben 36 Fragen beantwortet, z. B. wieviel Zeit sie im Internet verbringen, zu welcher Uhrzeit, [...] und ob sie schon andere in bezug auf die Zeit, die im Internet verbracht wurde, **belogen** haben.
'The participants in this study answered 36 questions, for instance: how much time do they spend on line, at what time (of day), [...] and whether they have deceived (lit. *be*-lied) others concerning time spent on-line.'

Unlike its ostensible English counterpart *lie*, *lügen* does not accept an oblique argument expressing the party deceived. The sentence **Er log mir über den Unfall* 'He lied me (dative) about the accident' is ill formed, as are the variants illustrated by **Er log auf/zu/gegen mich über den Unfall* 'He lied on/to/against me about the accident'. Therefore, the applicative verb in (1.3) could not be said to code as a direct argument what would otherwise be coded as an oblique (preposition phrase or dative). Instead, the applicative pattern itself appears to license the 'malefactee' argument. This licensing effect is not limited to that of merely INCREASING verbal valency. In our final class of cases, exemplified by (1.4), the input form has no valency (or, equivalently, argument structure); the base form is a noun rather than a verb:

(1.4) Message ID
<1998090913374500.JAA19465@ladder01.news.aol.com>
Es mag ja lustig sein, zwei hartgekochte Eier wie Clownsköpfe mit angekeimten Sojabohnen zu **behaaren** und sie auf Gurkenscheiben zu stellen, ihnen mit zwei Tomatenstreifen Münder zu verpassen und Auglein aus Sojasprossen einzudrücken.

[2]This is true at least for Southern German dialects; Northern German seems to have only the intransitive variant of the base verb (*schimpfen auf*), which is found in Southern German as well.

> 'OK, it might be funny to *be*-hair two hard-boiled eggs like clown's heads with germinating soy beans, to stand them up on cucumber slices, to give them mouths from tomato strips, and to impress soy shoots on them as little eyes.'

In (1.4), a trivalent applicative predication, the base form is the noun *Haar* 'hair'. This word is inherently nonrelational, and has no verbal counterpart outside of the applicative construction; there is no transfer verb **haaren* 'hair'. The applicative predication in (1.4) denotes a transfer event of the type denoted by trivalent applicative verbs like *laden* 'load', and yet the transfer implication cannot be attributed to the semantics of the base form, which in this case is not a verb, let alone a transfer verb. In all of the examples (1.1-1.4), the appropriate inputs are simply lacking.

In addition to calling into question the feasibility of an alternation-based model of the applicative pattern, the examples in (1.1-1.4) also disturb the neat picture of constrained productivity presented above. These examples suggest that the applicative pattern is in fact not particularly selective about its inputs. If this is so, it becomes far more difficult to describe what speakers know about the use of the applicative pattern. One could claim that the tokens in (1.1-1.4) are opaque to the extent that they do not bear on the function of the applicative; however, (1.1-1.4) illustrate productive uses. Applicative predications like the denominal in (1.4) are novel, and in fact many of the novel tokens used to illustrate the productivity of the German applicative involve base verbs which do not denote transfer, locomotion or location. Brinkmann (1997:11), for example, cites as evidence of the productivity of *be*-prefixation relatively unconventional attested tokens like *bestreifen* (a denominal verb meaning 'patrol an area' for which a verbal base form **streifen* 'patrol' is lacking) and *bedudeln* (roughly, 'drone someone'), whose base form is the intransitive verb *dudeln* 'play tunelessly'. Despite what Brinkmann implies in that discussion, these novel examples of *be*-prefixation have little relevance for the productivity of *the locative alternation*. If we assume that the productivity of a form is evidence of a specific function, and that the function of the applicative pattern cannot be 'locative promotion', then we face the challenge of discovering what function of *be*-prefixation accounts for both novel denominals like (1.4) and the examples typically used to illustrate the locative alternation.

Even were we to broaden the function of the applicative to that of promoting any argument otherwise expressible as a preposition phrase (and not merely a locative argument), we would run into difficulty. This analysis appears to be a valid one: certain bivalent *be*-verbs which do not qualify as verbs of location nevertheless have bivalent intransitive counterparts which license a prepositional phrase. Brinkmann (1997:84-85) points to several verb classes in which such alternations can be found, including verbs of active perception, verbs of speech, and verbs of emotional expression. Pairs exemplifying alternations in each class are, respectively, *riechen an/beriechen* 'sniff [e.g., a flower]/sniff thoroughly'; *sprechen über/besprechen* 'talk about/discuss'; and *weinen um/beweinen* 'cry about/mourn [e.g., a death]'. However, the broader alternation-based model would not extend to bivalent applicative verbs with transitive counterparts (e.g., *beschimpfen* in (1.2)) or to bivalent applicative verbs with monovalent counterparts (e.g., *bedudeln*). The latter class of verbs includes not only *belügen* in (1.3) but also applicatives formed from other verbs of deception, including *schummeln* and *mogeln* 'cheat' and *schwindeln* 'fib'. A fortiori, the broader conception of the applicative alternation does not encompass applicative verbs which lack verbal base forms entirely, e.g., *bestreifen* '*be*-patrol' and the denominal applicative *behaaren* in (1.4). Thus, even a very broad conception of the 'promotion' function of the applicative appears to be too narrow.

If we abandon the idea that the applicative pattern is an argument-promotion device, we might then ask whether it is used to achieve semantio-pragmatic effects that are not derivative of the promotion function. It would be a challenge to isolate and describe such effects, if they exist. The examples in (1.1-1.4) demonstrate that the range of meanings associated with *be*-prefixed verbs is fairly large, and includes an 'affectedness' implication (1.1), (1.3), an intensive-action implication (1.2), and a transfer implication (1.4). These examples raise the following two questions.

First, do these meanings have anything in common? Ironically, the very characteristic of *be*-prefixation which makes it worthy of an in-depth synchronic study—its high type frequency—also appears to point toward a bleached rather than rich semantics (Eroms 1980). The number of *be*-prefixed verbs is considerable: there are more than 500 such verbs in German. When a common semantic denominator is recognized, it is generally highly schematic. Wunderlich (1987), for example, proposes that *be*-predications express 'topological local proximity'. Others have proposed a general implication of 'affectedness' of the object-denotatum (Filip 1994). Both of these analyses seem plausible, and yet the implications in question can also be also be attributed to a semantic prototype for transitive predications (Hopper and Thompson 1980, Hopper 1985).

Second, if there are semantico-pragmatic properties common to *be*-predications alone, is *be*-prefixation itself responsible for those commonalities? While proponents of lexical-rule based approaches appear to agree that semantic constraints determine whether a linking rule can APPLY, most appear highly uncomfortable with the idea that a linking rule can CONTRIBUTE conceptual content not found in the input verb. Thus, Gropen et al. (1991) and Pinker (1989) argue that the connotation of 'affectedness' associated with oblique-promoting patterns is a general implication of direct-object coding rather than an implication contributed by the linking rule (see also Lebeaux 1988, Rappaport and Levin 1988, Tenny 1987). This position makes sense against the backdrop of an alternation-based model, in which linking rules neither create nor destroy any aspect of thematic structure. The effect of a linking rule is thereby limited to that of altering the expression of participant roles. Since the examples in (1.1-1.4) call into question the principle of conservation of thematic structure, they also call into question its corollary—the proposition that linking rules do not contribute meaning to predications.

In response to the first question, we argue that the various semantic implications of *be*-predications are related by virtue of evoking parts of a single semantic schema. However, the relevant commonalities cannot be captured by assuming a vague semantics—what Horn (1989) refers to as a MONOSEMY analysis. Such an analysis would be too abstract to account for those semantic features which make the prefix productive and which render less than fully conventionalized combinations, like *behaaren* (in (1.4) above), interpretable. In the semantic analysis which we propose, the commonalities among the usages of the *be*-pattern are captured through an associative network based on a semantic prototype (see Goldberg 1995, Lakoff 1987). Each sense in the proposed network represents a pairing of formal and semantic constraints. Each sense will be described in terms of its LINKING PROPERTIES, i.e., in terms of the relationship between thematic roles and grammatical functions that the particular sense involves. The senses may differ with respect to the number and kind of participant roles involved. However, in accordance with Lakoff's (1990) INVARIANCE HYPOTHESIS, we postulate that all metaphorically based extended senses inherit both thematic structure and a specific linking constraint from the central sense. The linking constraint associated with the central sense states that the locative (or goal) argument cannot be realized as an oblique grammatical function.[3]

---

[3]This solution is similar in its effect to Alsina and Mchombo's (1990) analysis of the Chichewa applicative, in which the 'dependent recipient' argument is prevented from receiving the coding appropriate for a [+r], i.e., restricted argument. However, as argued by Goldberg (1995:114), the LFG rules proposed fail as such because they are radically context sensitive—constructional—rather than general, as the theory requires.

We argue that the semantic schema which is conventionally associated with the applicative pattern is one in which a THEME physically covers a LOCATION (either over the course of time or at a given point in time). This meaning has been extended into metaphorical domains. The relationship between the literal meaning of the construction and these metaphorical extensions will be represented by links denoting metaphorical mappings (Goldberg 1995, Lakoff 1987). These links include the following independently motivated metaphorical mappings (Reddy 1979, Lakoff and Johnson 1980, Sweetser 1990, Goldberg 1995): DISCOURSE IS TRAVEL OVER AN AREA, PERCEIVING IS COVERING OBJECTS WITH ONE'S GAZE, THE CONDUIT METAPHOR, EFFECTS ARE TRANSFERRED OBJECTS. We further propose that, through a mode of grammaticalization called PRAGMATIC STRENGTHENING (Hopper and Traugott 1993, König and Traugott 1988), the applicative pattern has also come to express TRANSFER, ITERATED ACTION, INTENSIFICATION of the action or state denoted by the verb, and EFFECTS achieved by means of an action. These inference-based extensions conventionalize prototypical components of applicative semantics, while canceling entailments related to coverage. An analysis of this type will allow us to capture the notion that *be*-predications form a coherent semantic group, although a given pair of *be*-predications may differ greatly.

With regard to the second question, concerning the source of the semantic effects observable in *be*-predications, we argue that the meanings of examples like (1.1-1.4) are products of a reconciliation procedure in which the meaning of the verb is brought into conformity with the meaning conventionally assigned to the argument-structure pattern flagged by the prefix.[4] In this account, the *be*-prefix is a morphological requirement upon an ARGUMENT-STRUCTURE CONSTRUCTION, in the sense of Goldberg (1995). Such constructions are linking templates which denote basic-level event types (like transfer and caused motion). As Saussurean signs, such pairings are highly similar to verbs. Both verbs

---

[4] An anonymous reviewer has made us aware of a potential misunderstanding arising from our description of the prefix as 'flagging' a construction. We do not wish to imply that there really are two constructions, one of them the actual applicative having the coverage semantics we will argue for, and the other the applicative-flagging construction. The reasons are twofold. First, adopting this analysis would mean assuming that there are deadjectival and denominal verb entries that cannot be lexicalized, a notion we reject. Second, having *be-* flag verbs with an applicative meaning would force us to explain why *be-* doesn't combine with simplex verbs such as *tapezieren* 'wallpaper', *dekorieren* 'decorate', *pudern* 'powder', *schmücken* 'decorate' that have applicative meanings as well. As we will see in Chapter 4, the prefix *be-* is a piece of morphology that the applicative construction specifies; it is part of the construction, not separate from it.

and argument-structure constructions have (a) thematic and Aktionsart structure, (b) meanings which are subject to systematic extension, and (c) idiosyncratic usage constraints. The conception of grammar as a hierarchically organized inventory of form-meaning pairs (with greater and lesser degrees of internal complexity) is central to CONSTRUCTION GRAMMAR (CG) (Zwicky 1994, Kay and Fillmore 1999, Goldberg 1995, Michaelis and Lambrecht 1996, Jackendoff 1997b). CG is a monostratal theory based on unification of feature structures.

The metaphor of unification provides a model of argument structure distinct from that which underlies derivational accounts based on lexical rules. In the CG model of argument structure as proposed by Goldberg, the semantic effects observable in (1.1-1.4) do not result from 'derivations' in which a restricted set of 'input verbs' undergoes modification of semantics and syntax, whether in the lexicon or elsewhere. In the CG model, verbs do not have alternate semantic representations. Instead, verb meaning is constant across syntactic contexts. No additional lexical entry is created to represent the meaning and valence of verbs found in specialized patterns like the ditransitive. Instead, verbs unify with verb-level linking constructions which denote event types. These linking constructions assign grammatical functions to participant roles contributed by the verb. Since, however, these constructions denote event types, they have their own array of thematic roles, which may PROPERLY INCLUDE the set of roles assigned by the verb. In such cases, verbs which combine with the construction undergo modulation of their thematic and valence structure. Because the construction can augment the valence set licensed by the verb, the event type designated by a predication is not determined exclusively by the argument structure of the head verb. In the case of the applicative pattern in particular, as we will show, the construction not only AUGMENTS verbal valency but is also in the business of CREATING valence patterns for open-class items which are not inherently relational. We will attempt to demonstrate that the constructional account provides a more principled account of the productivity of the applicative pattern than do accounts based upon lexical rules.

While the sign-based approach to argument-structure admits both endocentric (head-based) and exocentric (non head-based) sources of thematic structure, we do not thereby abandon the central goal of lexical-licensing theories—to provide a compositional account of the relationship between verb meaning and sentence meaning. In the constructional account, the combination of verb and construction is modeled compositionally. Following Goldberg (1997, 1995: 65-66), we assume that the set of possible relationships between verb and construction denotata is highly constrained. The constructional approach entails a significant change in focus in the study of argument structure: we are no longer concerned with the 'alternations' that lexical rules have been used to represent, but instead with the inherent meanings of the linking patterns with which verbs combine.

This account also entails a shift away from models of productivity based upon a putative dichotomy between derived and stored word forms (as per Pinker and Prince (1991)). In Construction Grammar, as in other use-based models, word-formation principles are modeled as schemas rather than on-line processes. The productivity and, thereby, the extensibility of a schema is determined by its type frequency, as per Bybee (1995). Since the types which delimit the application of verbal linking patterns are verb classes, verb classes (i.e., stored items) provide the lens through which we may view the behavior of the linking pattern.

This monograph is structured in the following way. In chapter 2, we will discuss a recent account of the function of *be*-prefixation, presented by Brinkmann (1997) as part of an acquisition study of the locative alternation in German. Although the locative alternation has been widely described, we chose to react to Brinkmann's account because it is comprehensive in its attention to previous literature, provides a clear and well articulated example of the derivational approach to argument structure, and represents a strong challenge to the view advanced here—that the semantic effects observable in (1.1-1.4) are attributable to a specific formal pattern rather than to more general principles of linguistic interpretation. In chapter 3, we will more fully motivate the CG approach and discuss the advantages that this approach offers to the analysis of the relevant argument structure. Chapter 4 demonstrates the application of multiple linking constructions in the licensing of sentences. Chapter 5 discusses the semantic structure associated with the applicative pattern, its metaphorical and pragmatic extensions, and constraints on the productivity of the pattern as these relate to semantically defined verb classes. The appendix contains information on the data sources and a full listing of *be*-verb classes.

2

An Alternation-Based Account of the Applicative Pattern

2.1 Overview of Brinkmann (1997)

Alternation-based accounts of the meaning of the *be*-pattern tend to have the following two characteristics. First, they presume that an abstract derivation mediates between prefixed and nonprefixed lexical entries, where entries of the latter type are the 'input'. Second, they use general interpretive principles to account for the meanings of applicative sentences, rather than invoking constraints on the form-meaning correspondence that the applicative pattern represents. Accounts of this type include Pinker 1989 for the English locative alternation and Wunderlich 1987 for German *be*-verbs. Brinkmann's (1997) account, which is based on Wunderlich's (1987, 1991, 1997) work on prepositions and the complex semantics of German prefix verbs, also exhibits both of the above characteristics. First, within LEXICAL DECOMPOSITION GRAMMAR inseparable-prefix verbs that take locations as direct objects are lexically derived from their unprefixed base verbs through FUNCTIONAL COMPOSITION of a verbal predicate and a prepositional predicate. This process of PREPOSITION INCORPORATION is assumed to be a general grammatical mechanism, i.e. motivated beyond *be*-verbs, and largely neutral with respect to the semantics of the derived predicates. Second, all semantic effects characteristic of *be*-verbs are accounted for either by constraints on the verb classes that can participate in the alternation or by independently motivated semantic analyses, rather than via semantic constraints originating from the rule itself. In particular, the following general principles are argued to be involved in the interpretation of *be*-verbs. Brinkmann proposes the NONINDIVIDUATION HYPOTHESIS to account for the omissibility of the theme argument. Wunderlich's SATISFACTION CRITERIA, which are derived from Löbner's (1990) PRESUPPOSITION OF INDI-

VISIBILITY, are used to account for the so-called holistic effect on the referent of the direct object, i.e., the location.

We question both of these two fundamental components of Brinkmann's analysis. In the next section (2.2), we will point to three major weaknesses of the preposition-incorporation model. In section 2.3, we will question Brinkmann's claim that all specific semantic effects can be accounted for straightforwardly by reference to general interpretive principles and etymology. This section will focus on three interpretive features which characterize *be*-predications: the holistic interpretation of the goal argument, the omissibility of the theme argument, and the interpretation of the goal argument as a two-dimensional or planar region. For each of these three features, we will show that Brinkmann's putatively general account cannot in fact be interpreted coherently without reference to semantic effects associated directly with the linking pattern.

2.2 The Mechanism of Preposition Incorporation

Fundamental to the Brinkmann-Wunderlich account is the idea that the location argument becomes available for direct (i.e., nonoblique) case-marking via the amalgamation of two predicate-argument structures, that of the base verb and that of the bound prefix *be-*. We will suggest in section 2.2.1 that the apparatus used to represent this derivation considerably complicates the relationship between semantic and syntactic structure. In section 2.2.2 we will argue that the model is also unable to plausibly account for a fundamental feature of *be*-prefixation: its role as a valence-augmenting device. In section 2.2.3. we will point out that the model in its current form does not (as claimed) provide an account for all German prefix-verbs.

2.2.1 Grammatical Architecture

Here we will consider the means by which the decompositional account relates the semantic and syntactic structures of unprefixed verbs to those of *be*-verbs. Consider *sprühen* 'spray' and *besprühen* '*be*-spray, spray [a surface]'.

(2.5) Sie **sprühte** Farbe **an** die Wand.
'She sprayed paint on the wall.' (=Wunderlich 1997:29a)

(2.6) Sie **besprühte** die Wand mit Farbe.
'She sprayed the wall with paint.' (=Wunderlich 1997:29b)

According to Wunderlich's (1997:5) decompositional grammar, shown in Figure 2.2.1, these verbs lexicalize two different conceptual structures, as shown by their semantic form (SF) representations:

(2.7) {SPRAY(x,y) & P(y)}(s)
(2.8) {SPRAY(x,y) & BECOME (LOC(y, AT(z)))}(s)

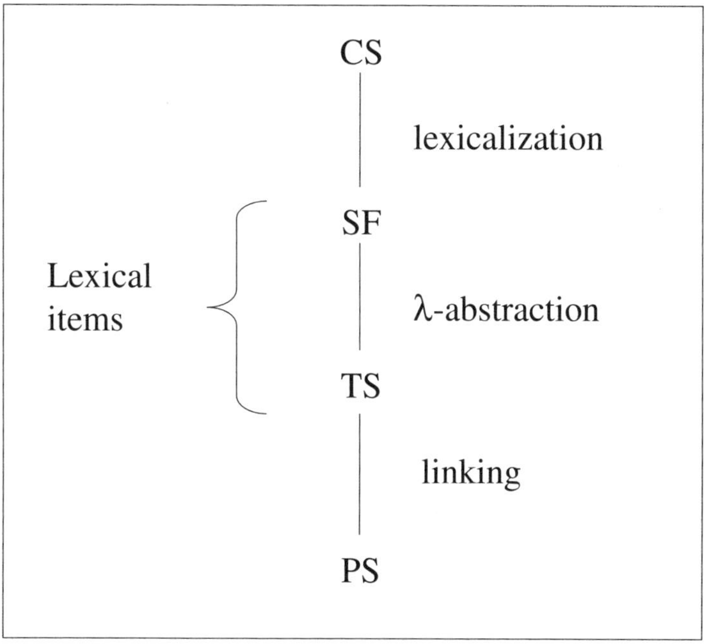

FIGURE 1 Lexical Decomposition Grammar

In (2.7-2.8), x is the agentive argument, y is the theme argument, z is the location argument, and s is a situation variable. The expression in curly brackets is an event type which is predicated of the variable s. Conjunction is assumed to be asymmetric, with the result that P(y) can be considered an internal argument of the conjunction and therefore more deeply embedded in the SF of *sprühen* than SPRAY (x,y). Via Wunderlich's Coherence Principle, the conjunction is causally interpreted (1997:36). In (2.7), the one-place predicate P is a variable over properties expressed by prepositional phrases (e.g., the property of being on the wall, as predicated of some paint). In (2.8), the operator BECOME is an inchoative operator which takes a location-state predicate (LOC) as its argument. The predicate LOC, in turn, takes two arguments: the theme and a two-place predicate AT, which is a variable over relationships expressed by prepositions (e.g., the relationship between some paint and the wall it is on). The difference between *be*-verbs and unprefixed verbs is modeled by assuming that in the case of the former (2.8) preposition incorporation occurs and the verb combines with a PREPOSITION (AT), which takes both the location and the theme as arguments, whereas in the case of the latter (2.7) the verb combines with a prepositional phrase (P). The predicate P takes only one argument, the theme. In other words, the location z is 'visible' to the representation in (2.8) but not in (2.7).

The level of SF is said not to determine surface syntax directly. As Figure 2.2.1 shows, a level of thematic structure (TS) intervenes between SF and the level of clausal syntax or phrase structure (PS). Wunderlich argues that TS is needed in order to account for three kinds of facts that cannot be read off SF directly (1997:43; 46-53). First, the occurrence of expletives with certain predicates cannot be predicted from conceptual structure (CS) or from SF. Second, lexical idiosyncrasies like 'quirky' case assignment do not follow from CS or SF. For instance, German *helfen* 'help' assigns dative case to the *helpee* rather than the accusative case that canonical transitive verbs assign to their objects. Third, voice operations such as passive result in argument linkings different from active-form verbs but one would not want to say that they are built on different SF representations, reflecting different conceptual structures. Thus, an additional layer of structure is needed to mediate between SF and phrase structure (PS). Thematic structure (TS) is that additional level; it is derived from SF by lambda abstraction. For our example verbs, lambda abstraction results in the following TS representations:

(2.9) $\lambda P \lambda y \lambda x \lambda s$ SPRAY(x,y) & P(y)(s)

(2.10) $\lambda z \lambda y \lambda x \lambda s$ SPRAY(x,y) & BECOME (LOC(y, AT(z)))(s)

In accordance with Bierwisch's (1988) Hierarchy Principle (see also Wunderlich 1997:34), the most deeply embedded arguments of the SF representations in (2.7) and (2.8)—the prepositional phrase P(y) and the location argument z—have become the highest arguments in TS in (2.9) and (2.10), respectively. That this reordering takes place has to do with the fact that, in contrast to ordinary λ-categorial syntax, lambda abstraction is stipulated within Lexical Decomposition Grammar to apply in a particular order. The motivation for this constraint is that the theory aims to constrain the semantic operations available in Categorial Grammar to those kinds that preserve the order of arguments, namely functional application and functional composition.

The linking of arguments to syntactic functions (and thence to morphological realizations) is specified by binary features attached to each argument in thematic structure. For each argument, the features specify whether there is a higher argument role [±hr] and whether there is a lower argument role [±lr]. Despite the fact that the binary features which drive syntactic-function assignment are associated with arguments at the level of thematic structure, the feature assignments themselves are based upon semantic form (predicate-argument structure), since they appeal to depth of embedding in semantic representation, rather than the reverse ordering found in thematic structure. Brinkmann (1997:91-92) provides the accomplishment verb *open* as an example. Its semantic representation is: CAUSE (x, BECOME (OPEN, y)). Accordingly, the theme receives the feature [+hr], since it is more deeply embedded in the representation than the agent. Structural case is assigned from these features in the following way: accusative case is assigned to an argument marked [+hr], dative case is assigned to an argument marked BOTH [+hr] and [+lr] and nominative is assigned to an argument which is marked [-hr] (by default in the case of single-argument verbs).

The application of the linking mechanism to the TS of our applicative verb *besprühen* (2.10) is straightforward with regard to the nominative and accusative arguments. The locative receives the assignment [+hr] and thereby receives accusative case. The agent receives the assignment [-hr] and thereby nominative case. A difficulty arises, however, when we come to the assignment of syntactic function to the theme argument, y. This argument must be marked [+hr, +lr] since in SF it is lower than the agent (x) and higher than the location (z). The argument y therefore ought to be realized as dative. But, as we know, it can only be realized in an optional oblique phrase. What accounts for the linking to oblique?

The answer is to make a further distinction between arguments that participate in structural linking and arguments that do not. This distinction relies on the notion of L-COMMAND. The notion of L-command is defined for hierarchical representations of logical types in SF. A representation of this type for *besprühen*, as given by Brinkmann (1997:98) is provided in Figure 2. L-command is defined for such structures in a way that is parallel to the definition of c-command for syntactic structures: 'a L-commands b iff the node g, which either directly dominates a or dominates a via a chain of nodes type-identical to g, also dominates b' (Wunderlich 1997:41). In addition, Wunderlich defines the notion of STRUCTURAL ARGUMENT: 'An argument is structural only if it is either the lowest argument or (each of its occurrences) L-commands the lowest argument' (loc. cit.). And, most importantly, only structural arguments are linked to grammatical relations through the system of features. As Figure 2 shows, the highest argument of *besprühen* is the sprayer, x. It is realized as nominative since it is marked [-hr]. The lowest argument is the location, z. It is marked [+hr, -lr] and is realized as accusative accordingly. By contrast, the theme argument of *besprühen*, y, is not a structural argument. This is so because y (a) is not the lowest argument

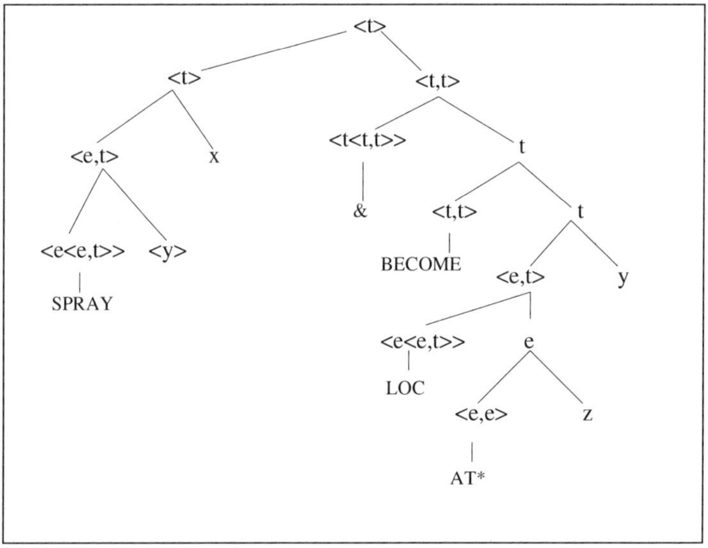

FIGURE 2 Hierarchical representation of logical types in SF of *besprühen* 'spray [a surface]'

and (b) fails to L-command z in one of its occurrences, that in which it is a sister to SPRAY. Since the theme cannot be expressed by a structural case, it must instead be linked by an oblique marker, in this case the preposition *mit* (Brinkmann 1997:99).

Since L-command is dependent upon the particular SF that is chosen, and since there may be a degree of latitude in the selection of the SF for a particular verb, the form of the SF representation may in practice be determined by the linking facts rather than vice versa. This problem arises in the case of trivalent verbs of transfer whose linking properties are distinct from those of the *be*-verbs. One such example is the verb *geben* 'give'. Wunderlich (1997: 60a) provides the following SF for *geben*: CAUSE (x, BECOME (POSS (y,z))). This SF maps to a hierarchical representation in which the recipient argument y L-commands the lowest argument, the theme, z. The recipient argument is the right sister of the type <e,t>, which dominates the predicate-argument pair POSS (z). The recipient is therefore a structural argument. It has the features [+hr,+lr]. Accordingly, we predict that the recipient argument will receive dative case, and this prediction is correct. In addition, we correctly predict from this representation that the theme will receive accusative case (it is marked [-lr]) and that the agent will receive nominative case (it is marked [-hr]).

However, the representation which Wunderlich provides for *geben* does not seem appropriate for trivalent transfer verbs like *senden* 'mail, send', which have linking properties identical to those of *geben*. While *geben* entails change of possession, *senden* does not entail reception of the theme—one can truthfully claim to have sent a package to someone prior to the recipient's having received the package. Further, sending involves a specific manipulation of the theme by the agent, and this activity should be represented in SF. If it were not, we could not obviously distinguish between different modes of transfer (sending, passing, handing, etc.). One would then have to ask why the manipulation involved in spraying, strewing, etc. is worthy of its own predicate in SF while that involved in sending, passing, etc. is not. In light of such considerations, we conclude that it would at least be plausible to represent *senden* by a SF analogous to that given for *be*-verbs: SEND (x,y) & BECOME (LOC (y, AT (z))). However, if we were to assume such a representation for *senden*, L-command would generate an incorrect result. In this representation, which is analogous to that in Figure 2, the first instance of the theme does not L-command the lowest argument (the goal). We would thereby predict that the theme would be realized as a nonstructural argument, and thereby by an oblique expression. Further, we would predict that the recipient receives accusative case (since it would be marked [-lr]). Both of these predictions are incorrect, since the recipient receives dative coding, and the theme is a structural argument, which receives accusative rather than oblique coding.

One could of course argue that the SF which we have provided for *senden* cannot be correct, since that SF is exclusively associated with verbs which have incorporated prepositions. However, this would be circular reasoning; if it is semantics which we are dealing with, then we need a *semantic* rationale for rejecting or accepting a given SF. If we hold SF constant for transfer verbs as a class, then capturing the difference between accusative and oblique themes appears to require recourse to stipulation. In fact, as we have seen, thematic structure does contain stipulations. Wunderlich proposes that the abstracted arguments in thematic structure 'are associated with syntactically relevant information: the category of the syntactic expression, the sortal restrictions imposed on the syntactic complements, the agreement features (Wunderlich 1994), and finally, the features regulating linking with case or with oblique prepositions' (1997:45). In other words, the oblique expression of the theme role appears to be a fact *about the applicative pattern*, rather than a fact which is independently motivated by semantic structure.

The relativization of linking constraints to particular linking patterns is seen as well in the analysis of passive. As mentioned above, Wunderlich views voice operations as an important motivation for a distinct level of thematic structure in lexical decomposition grammar. According to Wunderlich, passive 'removes the highest role ([-hr]) from the set of structural arguments, and it marks the lowest role ([-lr] otherwise) as [-hr] in the majority of languages' (Wunderlich 1997: 53, fn. 17). Thus, in a passive use of *besprühen*, the sprayer argument x is deleted from the hierarchy of structural arguments but is still available to be expressed as a nonstructural argument. The only remaining structural argument, the location z, must now be assigned [-lr, -hr]. This feature combination, as desired, can only unify with nominative. Again, however, these linking constraints are facts about the passive linking pattern, rather than facts which fall out from L-command or anything else.

The idea that linking constraints are idiosyncratic features of particular linking patterns is central to the constructional model. For this reason, we could not view the stipulation of linking constraints as a liability of any model. At the same time, however, we question the need for the ornate grammatical architecture which Wunderlich and Brinkmann rely upon. In accordance with Jackendoff (1983:14) we feel that it is appropriate to judge syntactic models according to the Grammatical Constraint. The Grammatical Constraint holds that a model which 'preserves a simpler correspondence of syntactic and semantic structure is to be preferred' over other models. The Wunderlich account makes the syntax-semantics interface very complex. First, it requires a stipulation concerning the order of lambda-abstracted arguments. Arguably, this stipulation is motivated only by the theory-internal preferences: to keep the relative order of arguments constant; to use a limited set of operations within Categorial Grammar; and to model what is taken to be emergent basic word order. Second, the argument hierarchy which is said to motivate the level of thematic structure (Brinkmann 1997:91) is in fact the thematic-role hierarchy in decompositional structure (SF), although thematic structure is claimed to be the interface level between SF and PS. While one may grant that thematic structure is a necessary level in that it expresses idiosyncratic feature linkings, these are stipulations which, as we have seen, contravene the generality of the model. Third, the account introduces the otherwise unmotivated concept of L-command to override the effects of structural linking where necessary. Since, as we have seen, hierarchical representations can be shaped to fit the actual linking facts, L-command appears to be derivative rather than predictive. Fourth, the decompositional account requires recourse to a highest-argument deletion operation and to rule ordering (highest-argument deletion before feature assignment and linking) in order to achieve the right interaction between the *be*-pattern and the passive linking pattern. In chapter 4, we will argue that this interaction can be modeled more economically through the unification of minimally specified linking constructions.

2.2.2 Representing Valence Augmentation and Creation

It stands to reason that a derivational account of argument structure, in which a lexical process changes the position in decompositional structure of argument roles, should require that the relevant argument roles be present in the input representation. This basic assumption is challenged by two large classes of *be*-verbs for which there is no appropriate input form: denominal, deadjectival and nonce *be*-verbs on the one hand and adjunct-promoting and valence-augmenting deverbal *be*-verbs on the other. We will discuss each of these two classes in turn, pointing to the additional layers of abstract representation which the Wunderlich-Brinkmann model requires for each class.

One may be tempted to extend the incorporation-based account of deverbal *be*-verbs to denominal and deadjectival *be*-verbs by assuming that a conversion mechanism derives simple verbs from the base adjectives and nouns before the regular preposition-incorporation mechanism applies. However, such an account lacks sufficient empirical support. First, there may be no simple verb that could be analyzed as the result of noun-verb or adjective-verb conversion. A case in point is the verb *beampeln* 'equip with traffic lights' in (2.11).

(2.11) www.schwerinonline.de/archiv/46-98.html
Die Kreuzung Arsenalstraße wird **beampelt**.
'The Arsenalstraße crossing will get equipped with traffic lights.'

There is no verb **ampeln* that derives from *Ampel* 'traffic light'. Second, even if there is a homophonous candidate verb, it may not have the appropriate meaning. This point is illustrated for denominal applicatives in our corpus by an on-line classified advertisement for a 24-needle flatbed printer in which the writer states:

(2.12) Er kann bis etwa 1mm starkes Papier oder Pappe **benadeln**.
'It can print on (lit. *be*-needle) paper or cardboard up to 1mm [thick]'.

There is a conventional source denominal *nadeln* but it is used of coniferous trees and means 'shed needles' rather than 'adding, placing needles', the required 'input' meaning for (2.12). Another example is the verb *beschildern* 'put up traffic signs' in example (2.13). It can be paraphrased accurately only by the predicate *aufstellen* 'put up' taking the argument *Schilder* 'traffic signs' as shown in example (2.14). A simple verb *schildern* exists but its meaning is 'describe', not 'put up traffic signs'.

(2.13) Message ID <4lq28k$lsr@nz12.rz.uni-karlsruhe.de >
Also *m.E.* regelt 41, wie ein Radweg zu **beschildern** ist und wer darauf was zu suchen hat und wer nicht, und dies unabhängig davon, ob der Radweg neben einer Straße liegt oder durch die Pampa führt.
'Well, *in my opinion* [paragraph] 41 regulates how a bike path needs to be equipped with traffic signs (lit. *be*-traffic-signed) and who has any business on it and who doesn't, and it does so independently of whether the bike path runs next to a street or through the middle of the prairie.'

(2.14) Also *m.E.* regelt 41, wie die **Schilder** auf einem Radweg **aufgestellt** werden müssen und wer darauf was zu suchen hat und wer nicht, und dies unabhängig davon, ob der Radweg neben einer Straße liegt oder durch die Pampa führt.
'Well, *in my opinion* [paragraph] 41 regulates how traffic signs have to be put up on a bike path and who has any business on it and who doesn't, and it does so independently of whether the bike path runs next to a street or through the middle of the prairie.'

Similarly the verb *befreien* in example (2.15) can be paraphrased most closely by the resultative construction *frei bekommen* 'get free, released' as shown by example (2.16). The simple verb *freien* means 'to woo' rather than 'to free, liberate'.

(2.15) *Süddeutsche Zeitung*, March 4, 1996
Deutsche Grenzschützer **befreiten** die Geiseln am 18. Oktober 1977 in Mogadischu; Andrawes überlebte als einziger der Terroristen.
'Members of the German border patrol freed (lit. *be*-freed) the hostages on October 18, 1977 in Mogadishu; Andrawes was the only one of the terrorists to survive.'

(2.16) Deutsche Grenzschützer **bekamen** die Geiseln am 18. Oktober 1977 in Mogadischu **frei**; Andrawes überlebte als einziger der Terroristen.
'Members of the German border patrol got the hostages free on October 18, 1977 in Mogadishu; Andrawes was the only one of the terrorists to survive.'

The lexical decomposition account seeks to deal with these kinds of *be*-predications by making two crucial assumptions. First, it allows for phonologically empty morphemes. In the case of denominals, empty verbs with appropriate meanings, such as 'put', simultaneously host preposition and noun incorporation processes.[5] In the case of deadjectivals, empty causative (CAUSE) and inchoative (BECOME) morphemes combine with the stative adjectival predicates to derive the right semantics. Second, the semantic input representations of deadjectival and denominal verbs are prohibited via stipulation from being lexicalized in another form. One may take issue with this approach on two counts. First, it seems rather *ad hoc.* Second, it does not explain what *be-* is doing in the formation of deadjectival *be*-verbs, since these verbs do not contain a stative LOCATIVE predicate.

There are also two kinds of DEVERBAL *be*-verbs which do not provide straightforward input representations. First, some verbs seem to incorporate an optional argument. For instance, in the case of *wachsen* 'grow' a location is not an obligatory complement; yet as shown in example (2.17), there is a verb *bewachsen* with a location object.

(2.17) Message ID <35fa4ec9.0@netnews.web.de>
SELBSTKLIMMER – Klctterpflanzen, die mit speziellen Haftorganen Wände oder andere Flächen direkt **bewachsen**, Beispiele: HAFTWURZELN bei Efeu HAFTSCHEIBENRANKEN bei Wildem Wein.
'Self-climbers = climbing plants that directly *be*-grow walls or other surfaces with the help of special adhesive/sticky extremities, for instance, sticky roots in the case of ivy, sticky tendrils in the case of wild vine.'

Wunderlich (1991:614) concedes that '[t]o describe this by functional application, we have to assume that the modifier[6] turns into an argument first, and then this argument is incorporated.' In other words, it is necessary to stipulate an additional operation and to order it before the derivation of the *be*-verb. Second, there are two classes of *be*-verbs whose unprefixed counterparts simply lack the arguments that appear with the *be*-verb. *Be*-verbs of the first class have related base verbs that do not allow the syntactic expression of the *be*-verb's (metaphorical) location argument. Consider the contrast between *mogeln* 'cheat, swindle' and *bemogeln*, shown in (2.18-2.19), respectively:

[5]This is the Wunderlich 1987 account. Though it is not entirely clear, Wunderlich 1997 may further decompose verbs like PUT into CAUSE (BECOME (LOCATED)).

[6]'Modifier' is Wunderlich's term for an optional verbal argument.

(2.18) Peter hat beim Kartenspielen **gemogelt**.
'Peter cheated in cards.'

(2.19) Peter hat mich beim Kartenspielen **bemogelt**.
'Peter cheated (lit. *be*-cheated) me in cards.'

While it is true that at the level of conceptual structure we may assume the existence of a victim of Peter's cheating in (2.18), this is irrelevant to the derivation of the *be*-form in (2.19). According to Wunderlich, argument shifting by morphological operation is only possible at the level of SF or at the level of TS (1997:52-53). At both of these levels, however, the location argument of *mogeln* is always absent. The second class at issue consists of deverbal *be*-verbs with arguments that arguably do not even exist on the conceptual level in the case of the unprefixed base verb.

(2.20) Message ID <6xulta5r4nB@link-m54.link-m.de>
Damals wäre um ein Haar ein Flüssiggastank in Mitleidenschaft gezogen worden [...] die Petershausner Feuerwehr mußte diesen daher intensiv **beregnen** [...]
'Back then a tank full of liquid gas almost got damaged [...] the Petershausen fire department therefore had to make a great effort to spray water on (lit. *be*-rain) it [...]'

The scenario of simple *regnen* 'rain' does not include an agent or cause of the precipitation:

(2.21) *Peter **regnete** die Blumen mit der Gießkanne.
'Peter rained the flowers with the watering-can.'

(2.22) *Das Gewitter **regnete** drei Tage lang.
The thunderstorm rained for three days.

Thus, there is not the right input available for the kind of derivation Wunderlich proposes. The problem of accounting for *be*-predications for which no source verb exists suggests strongly that the phenomenon at issue does not centrally involve operations on verbs, but instead the imposition of a particular valence-structure on a wide range of input lexical items.

2.2.3 Unpredicted Properties of Other Prefix Verbs

The preposition-incorporation model fails to predict the syntactic properties of several classes of prefix verbs. Consider the following data:

(2.23) Peter **spielte** den Ball **zu** mir.
'Peter played the ball to me.'

(2.24) Peter **spielte** mir den Ball **zu**.
'Peter played the ball to me (lit. to-played me the ball).'

(2.25) Der Notar **drückte** das Siegel **auf** die Urkunde.
'The notary stamped the seal onto the document.'

(2.26) Der Notar **drückte** der Urkunde das Siegel **auf**.
'The notary stamped the seal onto the document (lit. on-stamped the document the seal).'

The separable-prefix verb *zuspielen* 'play, pass theme [e.g. a ball] goal [recipient]' in sentence (2.24) looks very much as if it is derived from *spielen zu* 'pass/play [theme] to [goal]' in sentence (2.23). Similarly, *aufdrücken* 'impress' appears in example (2.26) to be derived from *drücken auf* 'press, stamp onto' in example (2.25). *Auf* and *zu* do not seem to be unusual prepositions and so preposition incorporation seems to be the natural way for relating the given pairs of verbs. However, the preposition-incorporation account does not correctly predict the case patterns of the prefixed verbs. Specifically, the account would not predict (a) that the theme arguments of the prefixed verbs (*Ball, Siegel*) are direct objects (rather than obliques); and (b) that the goal arguments of the prefixed verbs (*mir, Urkunde*) are obliques (rather than direct objects). Either the incorporation mechanism does not apply in the way it does for *be*-verbs or its effects can be overridden. In either case, the generality of the incorporation mechanism is diminished.

2.3 Interpretive Principles

Be-verbs have several idiosyncratic semantico-pragmatic properties. First, the goal argument seems to be affected as a whole by the action denoted by the verb (HOLISM). Second, the theme arguments of transfer scenarios can always be omitted (NULL COMPLEMENTATION). Third, the goal argument is always interpreted as a planar region rather than, say, a three-dimensional space (EXTERIORITY).

According to Brinkmann, these properties are not truly idiosyncratic. She argues that the first two are rather epiphenomena of more general syntactic and pragmatic principles and that the third follows from *be*-'s treatment as a bound preposition meaning 'on, at'. Contra these positions, we will argue in 2.3.1 and 2.3.2 that the suggested general principles cannot derive the intended semantics. In section 2.3.3 we will argue that the characterization of *be*- as a bound preposition meaning 'on, onto' is motivated only by considerations internal to the incorporation account and that it actually creates a conflict with the explanation given for holism.

2.3.1 Holism

Holism refers to the fact that the goal argument of a *be*-verb is construed as wholly affected by the action that the *be*-verb denotes. For instance, the sentence *Die Kinder bemalten den Tisch* 'The children *be*-painted/*be*-drew the table' evokes a scene in which there are drawings all over the table. This semantic characteristic of *be*-verbs is well known, and it is not specific to the German locative alternation: in the English sentence *John painted the table* it is similarly inferred that John painted all of the table surface. In his 1989 book on children's acquisition of argument structure, Pinker speculates that cross-linguistically the location-object members of the locative alternation always serve to encode the notion of affectedness of the location and that this common function makes the alternation learnable. However, Brinkmann shows convincingly that this cannot be true for German *be*-verbs. She points out, for instance, that it is not clear in what way the cake undergoes a change of state in example:

(2.27) Donna **bestreut** den Kuchen mit Zucker.
'Donna *be*-sprinkles the cake with sugar.' (=Brinkmann 1997:53a, p.71)

Similarly, she observes that in the case of *bewerfen* '*be*-throw' the theme need not even make contact with the goal or leave any visible traces. On the basis of such observations, Brinkmann concludes that affectedness understood as change of state cannot be a defining characteristic of German *be*-verbs. There is perhaps a more basic observation that renders Pinker's principle invalid: the affectedness implication is present whether the location argument is expressed as a direct object as in (2.27) or as a subject as in the case of the passive version of (2.27): *Der Kuchen wird von Donna mit Zucker bestreut* 'The cake is being *be*-sprinkled with sugar by Donna'. What is it then that gives rise to speakers' intuitions of holism concerning *be*-predications? Brinkmann argues that it is Löbner's (1990) PRESUPPOSITION OF INDIVISIBILITY.[7] Löbner's definition of the presupposition runs as follows: 'Whenever a predicate is applied to one of its arguments, it is true or false of the argument as a whole' [translation ours]. Applied to example (2.27), the principle predicts that coverage with sugar must be true for all parts of the surface of the cake, since *den Kuchen* is the direct object of the verb *bestreuen* 'strew'. Nothing needs to be said about affectedness of the cake.

While the indivisibility principle seems to work well for the above case, it cannot, as intended, be true for all predications—primarily because predication-argument relations are frequently metonymic (Fauconnier 1985, Lakoff 1987). Cases of what Jackendoff (1997a) calls ENRICHED COMPOSITION are clear exceptions to indivisibility. Consider,

[7] Brinkmann (1997) uses the term *indivisibility* to refer to what Löbner calls *holism*. We adopt the newer terminology.

for instance, uses of modifiers in which the modifiers do not apply in the expected way to their arguments. In what way does *sad* apply to *book* in *The book was sad*? Similarly, how does the predicate *begin* apply to *book* in *I began the book last night*? Even if we disregard this particular challenge for the moment, the indivisibility presupposition still faces problems. How would it apply, for instance, to the object of the verb *paint* in *John painted the living room door* if that door had a glass window in it? Would the glass not be part of the door proper? Even more importantly, what do we make of the fact that Brinkmann's cake sentence can be true even if the cake's surface shows through in some spots? From observations like these it follows that the indivisibility presupposition needs to be supplemented by more specific interpretive criteria. Wunderlich has suggested interpretive principles for locative verbs that denote an agent-initiated transfer of a theme onto a location. Consider the suggested satisfaction criteria for events of hanging pictures of Johnny Depp onto a wall:

(2.28) Wunderlich's Satisfaction Criteria

a. base verb: For all y: y is a picture of Johnny Depp => y is on the wall
b. *be*-verb: For all z: z is a sub-region of the wall => there is a y: y is a picture of Johnny Depp and y is located in z.

A sentence such as *Peter hängte Bilder von Johnny Depp an die Wand* complies with criterion (a) as long as there is more than one picture. The pictures may even be small in size. In order for a sentence with the corresponding *be*-verb to be true (i.e., *Peter behängte die Wand mit Bildern von Johnny Depp*) most of the wall must be covered with pictures of Johnny Depp. A large number of small pictures covering only part of the wall would not do, since Wunderlich's criterion (2.28b) calls for all sub-regions to be covered. At the same time criterion (2.28b) allows for the use of *be*-verbs in situations where not every part of the location is covered, as in the case of (2.27). This is possible because speakers are free to adjust the size of the sub-regions that must have something on them.

However, even after the addition of the satisfaction criteria there are still two problems with the presupposition of indivisibility. The first criticism concerns the specific formulation of Wunderlich's satisfaction criteria. It does not work for *be*-verbs like *beschiessen* 'put under fire, fire at' and *bewerfen* 'throw at'. As Brinkmann points out herself, one cannot assume that the theme will actually arrive on and impact the goal. It is perfectly reasonable to say, *Sie bewarfen uns eine Stunde lang mit Steinen, trafen aber keinen einzigen von uns* 'They *be*-threw us with stones for an hour but didn't hit a single one of us'. Therefore, the suggested satisfaction criteria are not applicable to cases like *bewerfen*: their semantics is unexplained. The second criticism concerns the fact that *be*-verbs overwhelmingly belong to one of the two classes of predicates that comply with the indivisibility presupposition rather than being more evenly distributed across the two classes.

The argument for the second criticism develops as follows. If the indivisibility presupposition is to have the status of a general constraint on predication,[8] it also needs to hold for sentences such as *Harry boxte Moe* 'Harry punched Moe'. However, under our current account it is not clear what the right subregions of Moe would be. To account for these cases, Löbner suggests that we refine our understanding of possible partitionings of an argument as follows. Predicates fall into two groups. On the one hand, there are SUMMATIVE predicates. A summative predicate applies to an argument if it also applies to each of the argument's parts.[9] To take Löbner's example, the sentence *The children are playing* could denote situations in which each child is playing his or her own game; situations in which groups of children play together; or situations where all children engage in a single game. On the other hand, there is the group of INTEGRATIVE predicates. Unlike summative predicates, these do not apply to arbitrarily chosen parts of the argument; in many cases they may not even apply to any parts at all.[10] There is only one admissible partition of the argument, the zero-partition; the argument must always be viewed as an undivided whole. Good examples of integrative predicates are ones denoting shape or weight. The sentence *The pieces of the puzzle form a rectangle* does not entail that each piece individually is rectangular or that arbitrary combinations of pieces form rectangles also. Another example of an integrative predicate is *knock-kneed*. If somebody is knock-kneed, it is strictly speaking only his or her legs that have this particular shape. Since one cannot pick body regions at random and predicate of them that they are knock-kneed, one has to classify the predicate as integrative. Now, based on the observation that the sentence *The children are playing*, which has a summative predicate, also has a

[8]We will ignore here the problem of enriched composition discussed above.

[9]'Ein Prädikat P mit einem Anwendungsbereich, in dem eine Teil-von-Relation definiert ist, ist genau dann summativ, wenn für alle i aus seiner Domäne und für alle zulässigen Aufteilungen A von i gilt:
P(i) = 1 gdw. [genau dann, wenn; JR and LAM] P(i') = 1 für alle i' aus A' (p. 25).

[10]'Integrative Prädikationen übertragen sich nicht von dem Argument auf beliebige Teile davon, in vielen Fällen sogar auf überhaupt keine echten Teile' (p. 25).

zero-partition reading under which all children engage in a single game, it is argued that integrative predicates are really just the limiting case of summative predicates. Understood in this way, integrative predicates then fall under the indivisibility presupposition.

However, now that we have determined that all verbs fall into one of two classes of 'indivisible' verbs we lack an explanation for the fact that the vast majority of *be*-verbs have a summative reading with respect to their location argument, even though they would also comply with the indivisibility presupposition if they had integrative readings. For instance, the verb *beladen* 'load' is summative: each part of, say, a truckbed must have a load on it. Yet, there is no principled reason not to expect transfer verbs like *beladen* to be integrative. Why couldn't, in Löbner's terms, the whole truckbed be viewed as the only relevant sub-region without being further divisible? In other words, why couldn't putting anything anywhere on the back of a truck be called *beladen*, since punching a person anywhere is punching that person?

As Löbner himself points out, one cannot determine whether a predicate is summative or predicative by looking at the argument: a person could be viewed holistically as the object of *punch* or as being composed of parts and regions as the object of *bespritzen* '*be*-splash'. Given that the semantics of the goal argument does not favor one kind of reading over the other and given that both summative and integrative predicates in principle comply with the indivisibility presupposition, we suggest that the *be*-pattern itself must be what gives rise to the summative readings of *be*-verbs.

2.3.2 Theme Omissibility

When a *be*-verb denotes a transfer scenario with an agent, theme, and goal, the theme can be omitted in surface syntax, i.e. null instantiated, when its referent is recoverable from context, as in (2.29):

(2.29) Die Jugendlichen **besprühten** die Wand (mit Farbe).
'The youths sprayed the wall (with paint).'

Brinkmann argues that this fact is predicted by what she calls the NON-INDIVIDUATION HYPOTHESIS. A theme is said to be nonindividuated if it is an unbounded mass or plexity, and is thereby not INCREMENTAL in the sense of Dowty (1991). When an entity is an incremental theme, each part of that entity is mapped to a temporal subpart of an event. The theme argument in (2.29), and other goal-object sentences, is non-incremental, i.e., nonindividuated. Properties of the theme argument (in particular its mapping properties) are not relevant to the determination of the endpoint of the event described, since it is wall space and not paint whose gradual exhaustion defines the time course of the spraying event in (2.29).

Brinkmann provides a general motivation for the nonindividuation of the theme argument in examples like (2.29), on the assumption that such predications denote processes. Accomplishment verbs, like *sing*, which otherwise select for an incremental theme, yield processual readings when their theme arguments are deindividuated, as in *I sang songs*. By the same token, she argues, the applicative pattern renders the theme's quantificational properties irrelevant by yielding a process reading of a verb like *laden*, which would not otherwise have one (p. 120). Examples of null-object complementation, e.g., *I read* or *She smoked*, are given as support for the idea that 'there is a close relationship between an incremental theme's omission from object position and its construal as nonindividuated' (p. 115).

While we concur with Brinkmann that nonspecific oblique themes of goal-object constructions are nonincremental, we will call into question two assumptions made by Brinkmann in her explanation of the nonindividuation hypothesis. The first assumption is that omissibility is determined by semantics alone. The second assumption is that nonindividuation of the theme—and thereby its omissibility—arises from a processual reading of the verb in an applicative construction. Let us now look at the way in which these two assumptions are expressed. Brinkmann gives the nonindividuation hypothesis two very different formulations. In the chapter on nonindividuation (chapter 4), the notion is defined as follows:

(2.30) The direct object of a transitive locative verb may be omitted only when the quantificational properties of the corresponding argument are irrelevant; the argument may then be existentially bound. (Brinkmann 1997:113)

The statement in (2.30) appears to be a necessary, and not sufficient, condition on omission of the theme argument: it restricts the conditions under which omission can occur ('the direct object may be omitted *only* when [...]'). However, it appears that (2.30) must be taken as a *sufficient* condition as well, since it is clearly intended as an explanation for the applicative linking. This explanation runs as follows: 'The theme does not need to be expressed syntactically, and this renders the object position available for the goal' (p. 249). In other words, (2.30) does not merely capture the observation that the theme arguments of trivalent applicatives are omissible; instead, it is intended as an answer to the question: 'Why do alternating transitive verbs allow the theme not to be expressed in object position?' (p. 248).

If we in fact take (2.30) as a sufficient condition on omission, there is a good deal that must be read into it. By 'direct object of a transitive locative verb' we assume that what Brinkmann intends is 'the argument which *would be* the direct object of a transitive *transfer* verb if the verb were not subject to the applicative linking, i.e., the theme'. In requiring that the quantificational properties of this argument be 'irrelevant', Brinkmann is presumably not targeting nonincremental themes in general but only nonincremental themes which could otherwise be incremental. Without the two provisos just mentioned, the condition might be taken as predicting omissibility in the case of a bivalent transitive verb like *enthalten* 'contain'. This verb appears to meet the conditions set out in (2.30): it is transitive, assigns a locative and a theme, and does not take an incremental theme. However, one could not explain one's failure to proffer a box by saying:

(2.31) *Die Schachtel enthält.
'The box contains [something].'

Appropriately adjusted, (2.30) predicts that in a spraying scenario like (2.29), where we have as much paint available as needed for coverage of the surface, paint need not be the direct object of *spray* and, in fact, may be omitted. This is just what we find. However, examples like (2.32) show that (2.30) cannot be a sufficient condition for omission. One cannot, for example, omit the theme object of a locative verb when the goal argument is linked to an oblique grammatical function.

(2.32) *Peter **lud auf** den Wagen.
'Peter loaded [something] onto the wagon.'

Thus, the literal interpretation of the nonindividuation hypothesis generates an incorrect prediction for unprefixed transfer verbs. As we have seen, Brinkmann treats oblique status and omission as two mechanisms for nonsyntactic expression. However, it appears that oblique status and omissibility are not the same thing. Instead, omissibility of the theme appears to be dependent upon oblique status, and capturing this fact requires that one refer to a particular linking. There is nothing in lexical decompositional grammar which would obviously allow one to do so, yet Brinkmann's formulation of the hypothesis does just that by referring to *direct object*, a grammatical function, and *quantificational properties*, a semantic notion. This mixing of levels is even clearer in Brinkmann's restatement of the hypothesis in her summary chapter:

(2.33) The nonindividuation hypothesis states that for a verb to take its goal as direct object, the quantificational properties of the theme must be irrelevant. The theme may then be construed as

> nonindividuated when it is not specified, i.e., as an unbounded amount of stuff or objects. (Brinkmann 1997:248).

Here Brinkmann refers expressly to *direct object* and *goal*—constructs which are located at different levels of decompositional grammar. The two formulations of the nonindividuation hypothesis also reveal a theoretical inconsistency. The second formulation is stated as a condition on the use of the *be*-pattern, while the first is stated as condition on argument omission. The second formulation makes sense only if it is restricted to trivalent *be*-verbs such as *besprühen* 'spray [a location]'. For bivalent *be*-verbs with theme subjects, e.g., *bewandern* 'hike around in'; *bewohnen* 'inhabit'; and *besetzen* 'occupy', it is not coherent:

(2.34) Peter **bewanderte** den Schwarzwald.
'Peter *be*-wandered the Black Forest.'

(2.35) Peter **bewohnt** ein Apartment.
'Peter inhabits (lit. *be*-lives) an apartment.'

(2.36) 5939806
Am Wochenende mußten 7000 Heilsuchende davon abgehalten werden, Nachbargrundstücke zu **besetzen** und Straßen zu blockieren.
'On the weekend 7000 patients had to be prevented from occupying (lit. *be*-sitting) neighboring properties and from blocking streets.'

It is difficult to determine whether Brinkmann views (2.33) as a general condition on *be*-prefixation. She relativizes most statements of the nonindividuation hypothesis to trivalent applicatives, and throughout her analysis treats bivalent theme-subject applicatives only in passing. If (2.33) were to be construed as such a condition, it would not obviously extend to examples like (2.34-2.36). These examples have a goal object, and the theme argument, the subject, is nonincremental. However, there is no sense in which this theme argument is or could be nonindividuated, since in each case the theme argument is a referentially specific entity. Clearly, (2.33) cannot express a general constraint on *be*-prefixation. The principle therefore fails to capture a crucial feature that the bivalent examples in (2.34-2.36) and trivalent examples share: the locative is the argument whose quantificational properties are relevant. A critical number of its subparts must be occupied by a theme or themes either through time (as in (2.34)) or at a given time (as in (2.35-2.36)).

But even if we grant that the function of the applicative pattern is deindividuation of the theme, and limit ourselves to the trivalent cases, it seems implausible to suggest that this deindividuation (and thereby omissibility) of the theme comes from a processual reading of the verb.

Omission of the theme argument of an incremental-theme verb does not entail a processual reading for that verb. For example, a predication like *I ate* is compatible with an *in*-phrase of duration—a hallmark of telicity—in examples like *I ate in 5 minutes so I wouldn't be late.* But perhaps more importantly, sentences like (2.29) simply do not denote processes; they denote bounded causative events, i.e., accomplishments. Brinkmann recognizes that the processual analysis of such tokens appears at odds with the interpretive facts. However, she points out (p.119) that the transitions denoted by trivalent applicatives, like that of a wall becoming covered with paint, do not take place abruptly but are instead the result of a process. Therefore, she concludes, goal-object sentences 'denote a process that leads to a transition' (p. 119).

This claim of course is compatible with the general analysis of accomplishment predicates in decomposition-based models (e.g., Bickel 1997, Foley and Van Valin 1984). But if the 'output' verb (applicative) incorporates a process predicate, the 'input' verb incorporates the very same one. In what sense, then, can one say that a processual reading has been added in the case of the applicative? In addition, as Herweg (1991) demonstrates convincingly, entailing a process and being a process are two different things. If this were not so, he argues, accomplishment predications would share with activity predications the entailment pattern which he refers to as the DISTRIBUTIVITY PROPERTY (i.e., the subinterval property as per Bennet and Partee (1978)). Accomplishment predicates demonstrably lack the distributivity property. Further, predications like (2.29) fail tests for atelicity and pass tests for telicity, in particular tests involving durational-adverb selection. It makes sense that this should be so, since the locative argument, as Brinkmann herself acknowledges (p. 121), provides the 'measuring out' function that serves to delimit the event.[11]

Finally, one must wonder why, in a model of the locative alternation based on lexical decomposition, there is no representation of the aspectual transformation which Brinkmann proposes. Perhaps such a representation would be incompatible with the model. An advantage claimed for the preposition-incorporation account over accounts based on affectedness is that '[it] shows how we can explain the locative alternation without positing that the verb changes its meaning' (p. 248). If no meaning change occurs, in what way can we interpret Brinkmann's claim that the applicative provides a mechanism for 'turning the verb into a predicate that specifies a process' (p. 120)? The processual reading

[11] Not all trivalent applicative predications are telic, as we will demonstrate in section 5.1.

cannot be a function of the deindividuated construal of the theme, since allowing this would create circularity: the deindividuated construal of the theme is in fact claimed to be dependent upon the processual reading of the verb.

In sum, we have seen that the quantificational properties of the theme argument do not provide a sufficient condition for the omission of that argument and that the omission of the theme argument in trivalent applicatives cannot plausibly be attributed to a processual interpretation. Insofar as this is the case, omissibility of the theme argument appears to be a function of a particular linking (to oblique), and not of a general principle.

2.3.3 Exteriority

The only semantic fact about *be*-verbs which Brinkmann attributes directly to the prefix *be-* is the restriction that the goal argument must denote the exterior of an object (pp. 81-82). This constraint is illustrated by the ill-formedness of (2.38) when intended as a paraphrase of (2.37). The only acceptable interpretation for example (2.38) is that in which the seeds are thrown at the outside of the garbage can rather than inside it:

(2.37) MessageID <667b0LdWeWB@p-ej.link-h.comlink.apc.org>
Bin auch für Kernkraft! Überlegt einmal, wieviel Kerne wir täglich **in** den Mülleimer **werfen**, ausspucken oder verschlucken, ohne ihre Kraft zu nutzen.
'I am for nuclear power, too ! Just think how many seeds (lit. nuclei) we throw into the garbage can, spit out or swallow every day without using their power.'

(2.38) Bin auch für Kernkraft! Überlegt einmal, mit wievielen Kernen wir täglich den Mülleimer **bewerfen**, wieviele wir ausspucken oder verschlucken, ohne ihre Kraft zu nutzen.
'I am for nuclear power, too! Just think with how many seeds a day we *be*-throw the garbage can, how many we spit out or swallow without using their power.'

Be-, like other inseparable prefixes of German, has no corresponding free form that can be used as a preposition or particle. As Brinkmann points out, *be-*'s closest living relative is the preposition *bei*, which is related to English *by* and has a meaning of 'by, close, near, at'. In none of its uses does *bei* involve contact between a theme and a landmark. Therefore, *be*-verbs cannot be formed—synchronically at least—by incorporating *bei*. Brinkmann points out that *be*-verbs can be used to paraphrase unprefixed verbs with goal expressions that are either encoded by *auf* 'on [horizontal surface]' as shown in (2.39) and (2.40) or by *an* 'on [vertical surface]' as shown in (2.41) and (2.42). Both of these prepositions have the needed meaning element 'contact with a surface'.

(2.39) Ted **schmierte** Butter **auf** die Tischdecke.
'Ted smeared Butter onto the tablecloth.'

(2.40) Ted **beschmierte** die Tischdecke mit Butter.
'Ted smeared (lit. *be*-smeared) the tablecloth with butter.'

(2.41) Petra **hängte** Sterne **an** den Christbaum.
'Petra hung stars onto the Christmas tree.'

(2.42) Petra **behängte** den Christbaum mit Sternen.
'Petra hung (lit. *be*-hung) the Christmas tree with stars.'
(= Brinkmann 1997:5, p.80)

Based on this analogy, Brinkmann introduces into the analysis a preposition *be* with the same predicate-argument structure as the preposition *an* 'on, onto'. The only difference is that *be* is a bound morpheme that cannot occur anywhere else but in *be*-verbs. This analysis may be historically plausible, and elegant in terms of the preposition-incorporation account, but its attractiveness is diminished by its idiomaticity—a particular lexical entry is created solely for the purpose of preserving a compositional account.

Further, even if we ignore the issue of incorporation and take the *be*-as-bound-*an/auf* analysis at face value, we run into a problem. For if the meaning of the bound preposition be corresponds to that of the prepositions *an* and *auf*, why then are *be*-verbs not synonymous with *an*- or *auf*-verbs derived from the same base? Consider the following pair of example sentences. While the *be*-sentence implies coverage of the whole tablecloth the sentence with the separable prefix in *an*- does not.

(2.43) Ted **beschmierte** die Tischdecke mit Butter. (= (2.40)

(2.44) Ted **schmierte** die Tischdecke mit Butter **an**.

If one assumes with Brinkmann that both verbs are formed by the same process of preposition incorporation, that the prepositions involved correspond to each other very closely semantically, and that syntactic principles such as indivisibility hold, then one would predict that sentence (2.44) means the same thing as sentence (2.43), or at least that the two sentences do not differ in ways that are controlled by compositional semantic principles. Yet, we find just that to be the case: only the *be*-sentence in (2.43) has the expected holistic reading.

This latest finding should not come as a surprise. We have seen on several occasions that even if one grants all the premises of each part of the Brinkmann-Wunderlich analysis, the resulting account still does not explain all the facts. Recall that Brinkmann's principles appear to be problematic when taken as general principles. The indivisibility principle, for instance, by its very generality fails to predict that *be*-verbs have summative readings rather than integrative readings. Similarly, the decompositional syntactic account of the argument-structure pattern fails to extend to *auf*- and *zu*-prefix verbs and *be*-verbs that involve valence creation, such as *beregnen* 'water, rain on'. These facts suggest strongly that rather than trying to derive the semantic and syntactic features of *be*-predications from general principles, one should attribute them to semantic constraints originating in a linking pattern to which *be*-predications conform. In the next chapter, we will outline a syntactic model which accords a central place to such patterns, beginning with a consideration of the philosophical context against which the constructional model of argument structure defines itself.

3

The Constructional Approach to the German Applicative

What would it mean to adopt a constructional rather than a lexical model of the applicative pattern? We will address this question in steps. Section 3.1 will describe the nature of the challenge that Construction Grammar has offered to the principle of lexical licensing, discuss the constructional model of argument structure and describe the constructional account of the German applicative pattern. This account rests on the assumption that the valency of verb and construction may differ. In sections 3.2-3.3.6, we will apply the model to five features of the pattern that proved troublesome for the Brinkmann account. Finally, in section 3.7 we will address two interrelated questions: to what extent does the constructional model adhere to Jackendoff's (1983) Grammatical Constraint and to what extent can it be described as compositional?

3.1 Theory Overview

The principle of lexical licensing holds that the basic scene denoted by a sentence (the set of participant roles expressed) derives from the argument structure of the head verb. Thus, for example, it appears clear that a sentence like *We gave the account to her* denotes a scene of transfer involving an agent, a theme and a goal because the semantic frame associated with the head verb *give* denotes a scene of transfer, and likewise requires the presence of these three participants. This principle is intrinsic to a compositional theory of semantics—a theory which has been seen as central to any account of syntax-semantics isomorphism, including that of Jackendoff, who states: 'It is widely assumed, and I will take for granted, that the basic units out of which a sentential concept is constructed are the concepts expressed by the words in the sentence, that is, lexical concepts' (1990:9). A more recent version of this principle is stated by Jackendoff as the principle of syntactically transparent composition: 'All elements of content in the meaning of a sentence are found in the lexical conceptual structures of the lexical items composing the sentence' (1997:48).[12]

The lexical-licensing principle has been central to the description of argument structure in most formal theories. Many such theories (e.g., Lexical Functional Grammar as described by Bresnan 1994 and Role and Reference Grammar as described by Van Valin and Lapolla 1997) posit universal linking rules, which capture generalizations concerning the syntactic realization of thematic roles assigned by verbs or verb classes (e.g., the class of transfer verbs). Such theories are driven by the assumption that 'argument roles are lexically underspecified for the possible surface syntactic functions they can assume' (Bresnan 1994:91). Universal linking rules map these argument roles to grammatical and pragmatic functions, and these rules do not add to, subtract from or alter the array of thematic roles associated with the verb. For example, in Bresnan 1994, locative inversion in English and Chichewa is represented as one linking possibility for verbs like *stand*, which subcategorize for locative and theme arguments. Such verbs are subject both to the linking rule which produces the configuration in (3.45) and to the linking rule which produces the configuration in (3.46):

(3.45) Two women stood in the plaza.

(3.46) In the plaza stood two women.

The syntactic structures of (3.45) and (3.46) are equivalent to argument-structure frames associated with the verb *stand*. However, the assumption of lexical licensing here makes it difficult for Bresnan to account for examples of locative inversion like (3.47), which involve an interpretive

[12]This more recent compositional principle is framed within a model which allows for an enriched conception of composition. In the enriched conception, the principle of syntactically transparent composition is treated as a default. The extended conception of composition allows for cases in which material that is not expressed by lexical items of the sentence may nevertheless be part of the conceptual content of the sentence. These are cases of coercion, in which extra meaning is 'added' in order to achieve well-formedness in conceptual structure and/or to 'satisfy the pragmatics of the discourse or extralinguistic context' (1997:49). For example, the 'iteration' feature is added to a sentence like *I blinked for two minutes* because a single blink cannot plausibly be viewed as lasting two minutes. The problem with Jackendoff's analysis, as we see it, is that coercion does not seem to have anything to do with the meaning of the syntactic pattern employed; Jackendoff does not posit a locus of association between semantic properties and syntactic form, i.e., a construction. For this reason, it would seem that coercion phenomena described by Goldberg (1995) and discussed in this section could not be easily handled by Jackendoff's coercion principle—the verb meaning is not modulated by particular co-occurring words or phrases, but by the particular linking configuration with which the verb integrates.

phenomenon which, following Talmy 1988, we will refer to as IMPLICIT CONVERSION:

(3.47) Through the window on the second story was shooting a sniper.

Examples like (3.47) are problematic in Bresnan's framework because the verb *shoot* does not assign either a locative role or a theme role, and yet it can appear in the locative-inversion configuration. In examples like (3.47), Bresnan argues, a locative-theme argument structure imposed by the pragmatic requirement of presentational focus is superimposed on the argument structure associated with the unergative verb *shoot*. The agent role of *shoot* will consequently be identified with the 'overlay theme' (p. 91). The problem with this type of account is simply that it is not explicit. If argument structures are products of the linkings licensed by given verbs, and not independent form-meaning pairings, it is difficult to understand the source of the 'overlay theme'.

Adherence to the lexical-licensing principle results not only in ad hoc devices like an 'overlay theme' in cases like (3.47), but also, as Goldberg points out (1995:9ff.), appeal to implausible verb senses. Goldberg discusses examples like the following:

(3.48) Most likely they were fellow visitors, just panting up to the sky-high altar out of curiosity. (Lindsey Davis, *Last Act in Palmyra*, p. 28)

(3.49) As they had waved us along the raised causeway and into the rocky cleft [...] (op. cit., p. 31)

(3.50) They can't just analyze away our data.

Goldberg points out that on the assumption that argument structure is determined exclusively by head verbs, we would need to assume the existence of a special verb sense for each of the usages exemplified in (3.48-3.50). Sentence (3.48) would require a special sense of *pant* equivalent to the formulation 'move while panting'; (3.49) would require a special sense of the verb *wave* whose definition would be 'signal permission to move to a place by waving'; and, finally, sentence (3.50) would require one to view *analyze* as a verb which denotes (metaphorical) caused motion. Such word senses, as Goldberg points out are not only ad hoc and unintuitive, but also compatible only with an assumption of radical and unconstrained polysemy.

Crucially, as Goldberg as well as Fauconnier and Turner (1996) have demonstrated, examples like (3.48-3.50) cannot easily be viewed as marginal or special cases. Sentence (3.48), for example, exemplifies a lexicalization pattern—conflation of manner and motion—which Talmy (1985) and Slobin (1997) have shown to be strongly entrenched in Germanic languages. Further, the examples in (3.48-3.50) cannot be regarded merely as violations of selectional restrictions associated with the verbal heads—or even as violations which might trigger manner-based implicata. If, for example, sentence (3.50) merely exemplified a violation of the selectional restrictions associated with the verb *analyze*, we would fail to predict its well-formedness—let alone the uniformity of its interpretation across speakers; (3.50) is necessarily interpreted as denoting metaphorical caused motion.

Cases like (3.48-3.50) give strong evidence that the principle of lexical licensing, despite providing a parsimonious account of transparent cases like the example involving *give*, is invalid. The alternative, construction-based model of argument structure outlined by Goldberg is founded on a body of work, of which Talmy 1988 is representative, which focuses on universal differences in the inventory of concepts expressed by open- versus closed-class elements, and in particular on the nature of the semantic interaction between grammatical and lexical elements. Crucially, grammatical constructions are viewed as belonging to the general set of meaning-bearing grammatical elements, which includes prepositions and derivational markers, among others. An essential tenet of these works is expressed in (3.51):

(3.51) OVERRIDE PRINCIPLE. If lexical and structural meanings conflict, the semantic specifications of the lexical element conform to those of the grammatical structure with which it is combined.

Zwicky proposes a similar universal interactional principle, which he relates to Panini's Law, since it involves the specific taking precedence over the general: 'Requirements in an evoking rule override those in an invoked rule' (1989:304). In acknowledging the applicability of (3.51) to cases like (3.48-3.50), we embrace the view that linking patterns are meaningful—that is, that they contribute schematic semantic structure distinct from that contributed by the verbs with which those patterns integrate. As grammatical constructions, linking patterns are complexes of formal, semantic, and pragmatic specifications. On this view, we would expect linking patterns to exhibit idiosyncratic constraints. For example, we would expect that semantic constraints above and beyond those on the theta frame of the input verb would be relevant for determining the applicability of a given linking pattern. These finer-grained constraints might include constraints on the pragmatic role or semantic type of certain arguments. A prominent topological restriction on the semantic of the *be*-pattern was discussed in section 2.3: *be*-predications, as Brinkmann observes (1997:81) 'describe motion to the exterior of an object'.

The constructional analysis of argument structure offered by Goldberg (1995, 1997) is founded on the assumption that linking patterns, like word lemmas, are 'directly correlated with one or more semantic structures' (1997: 383). Among the linking patterns considered by Goldberg are the ditransitive pattern (whose core semantics she captures with the formula 'X CAUSES Y TO RECEIVE Z'), the caused-motion pattern ('X CAUSES Y TO MOVE WITH RESPECT TO Z') and the resultative pattern ('X CAUSES Y TO BECOME Z'). Examples of each of these patterns are given in (3.52-3.54):

(3.52) We gave her the account.

(3.53) She put the checkbook on the counter.

(3.54) We painted the walls white.

Goldberg uses the term *sentence type* to refer to these linking patterns. In accordance with Fillmore and Kay (1997: ch. 8), however, we will regard linking patterns not as sentence structures but as verb-level constructions, which unify with the lexical entries of verbs. This unification has the effect of augmenting what Fillmore and Kay refer to as the MINIMAL VALENCE of the verb (the repertoire of semantic roles inherent to the meaning of the verb). The FULLY SPECIFIED verbal valence which results from unification of a verb's lexical entry with one or more linking constructions is one in which each semantic role is assigned a grammatical function.

Crucial to Goldberg's account is the idea that the repertoire of thematic roles assigned by the linking construction may PROPERLY INCLUDE the repertoire of thematic roles in the verb's minimal valence. In (3.55-3.57) we give examples of this phenomenon for each of the linking patterns exemplified in (3.52-3.54):

(3.55) We painted them a landscape.

(3.56) She blew the dust off the picture.

(3.57) We cried our throats ragged.

The verb *paint*, a verb of creation, denotes a two-place relation, involving the creator and a created item. However, sentence (3.55), an instance of the ditransitive linking pattern, adds an additional participant to the creation scenario—a potential recipient. This recipient is not intrinsic to the creation scenario; it is instead intrinsic to the transfer scenario with which the ditransitive pattern is associated. Likewise, while the verb *blow* is a one-place relation, involving an agent, (3.56) adds two additional participants—a theme and a goal. These participants are intrinsic to the caused-motion construction which the sentence instantiates. Finally, in (3.57), the verb *cry* appears with two more participants than it ordinarily has—a patient and a resultant state. The additional participants are licensed by the resultant-state construction that licenses (3.54).

The examples in (3.55-3.57) strongly resemble the examples in (3.48-3.50), which were used to undermine the validity of the lexical-licensing principle. Both sets of examples involve implicit conversion. We can regard linking patterns like the ditransitive and caused-motion patterns as CONCORD constructions. The theta frames associated with these patterns may, and indeed typically do, match those licensed by the particular verbal head. Examples of concord, given in (3.52-3.54) are those which provide the motivation for the lexical-licensing principle. Goldberg (1997) refers to these kinds of examples as instances of ELABORATION, in which the verb codes a more specific instance of the scene designated by the construction.

Examples of implicit conversion, given in (3.48-3.50) and (3.55-3.57), illustrate, as Goldberg points out, that while the head verb typically does elaborate the meaning of the construction, there are other relations that the verb may bear to the construction. A prominent relation, both across constructions and languages, is MEANS: the verb may code the means by which the action designated by the construction occurs (Goldberg 1995, 1997). Examples of the means relation are given in (3.56-3.57), in which, respectively, blowing is described as the means by which the dust is moved from one location to another and crying is the means by which the hoarseness is effected. The means and elaboration relations are mutually exclusive. The means relation is operative only when the theta frame associated with the construction properly includes that of the verb.

We view the *be*-pattern, whose formal representation will be given in chapter 4, as a transitive linking pattern like those exemplified in (3.52-3.54). Full consideration of its semantic and linking constraints will be delayed until chapters 4 and 5; it is sufficient here to say, as in the introduction, that it denotes thorough coverage of a location by a theme. This general semantic scenario is compatible with two more specific scenarios, which we will regard as minimal variants of one another: a trivalent causative scenario, in which an agent is present along with locative and theme, and a bivalent scenario entailing only theme and locative. The two versions of the construction differ only with regard to their semantic valency: the trivalent licenses the theta frame <agent, theme, locative> whereas the bivalent licenses the theta frame <locative, theme>. While the bivalent version INSTANTIATES the coverage scene, the trivalent ENTAILS that scene, in that an agent effects coverage. This semantic intersection is reflected in the sharing of single linking constraint: the locative is nonoblique. This situation is parallel to that described by Michaelis (1993) for Latin, in which entailment relationships between paired situation types, e.g., those of removal and lacking, are syntactically reflected in a shared linking constraint: the theme is ablative or genitive.

We will use the trivalent version of the *be*-pattern to exemplify the semantic interaction between construction and verb. Following Goldberg (1995:50), we will use the term FUSION to refer to the mechanism by which interpreters infer coreference relationships between arguments of the construction and participant roles assigned by the verb, where the latter are more specific instances of the former. We will assume, also in accordance with Goldberg (1995:65), that fusion is constrained by the Shared Participant Condition: at least one argument role of the construction must be fused with a participant role assigned by the verb. The verb may bear a means relation or an elaboration relation to the constructional semantics. Sentence (3.58) is an example of elaboration, while sentence (3.59) is an example of the means relation:

(3.58) Sie **belegte** den Stuhl mit ihren Büchern.
'She *be*-laid the chair with her books.'

(3.59) MK1/WPE.00000, PÖRTNER, DIE ERBEN ROMS, Roman
Auch die Höhen um Fulda **bebauten** die Mönche des frühen Klosters mit Kapellen, Kirchen und Propsteien.
'The monks of the early period of the monastery also *be*-built the hills around Fulda with chapels, churches, and provosts' residences.'

Example (3.58) exemplifies the elaboration relationship: the theta frame licensed by the trivalent verb *legen* is identical to the constructional theta frame. Example (3.59) exemplifies the means relationship between the bivalent verb *bauen* and the trivalent constructional theta frame. In this instance of the applicative construction, the agent role of the construction is fused with the builder role of *bauen* and the theme role of the construction is fused with the patient (factitive theme) role of *bauen*. The location role is unfused, since it is assigned by the construction alone. In the resulting predication, the verb, which denotes the creation of a structure, simultaneously denotes the means by which coverage (of the landscape surrounding Fulda) is effected. The reconciliation of verb and constructional semantics requires the inference that multiple buildings have been built, since only on this understanding is coverage entailed.

By assuming a constructional account of argument structure, we account not only for such reconciliation effects but also for all other features of *be*-predications which are not proper to input verbs. These are precisely the putatively noncompositional features of *be*-predications that proved troublesome for the Brinkmann account. For each, we will consider the alternative account offered by a construction-based model. The phenomena to be considered are: null complementation, valence augmentation, valence creation, the exteriority constraint, and the holistic-goal constraint.

3.2 Null Complementation

An essential problem for the Brinkmann account, as discussed in section 2.3, is that the pattern of null complementation licensed by *be*-predications cannot be predicted from the constraints on the 'input' verb. The null complementation possibilities licensed by verbs bearing the *be*-prefix are in fact the inverse of their nonprefixed counterparts, as demonstrated by the four-way comparison in (3.60-3.61):

(3.60) a. Er **sprühte** *(Farbe) **an** die Wand.
'He was spraying *(paint) on the wall.'
b. Er **sprühte** Farbe (**an** die Wand).
'He was spraying paint (on the wall).'

(3.61) a. Er **besprühte** *(die Wand) mit Farbe.
'He was spraying (lit. *be*-spraying) *(the wall) with paint.'
b. Er **besprühte** die Wand (mit Farbe).
'He was spraying (lit. *be*-spraying) the wall (with paint).'

This comparison shows that the *be*-pattern in (3.61) licenses a null theme argument while disallowing null instantiation of the locative argument, whereas the nonprefixed pattern in (3.60) shows the inverse pairing of constraints. It is further evident that the null complementation possibilities for locative in (3.60b) and theme in (3.61b) cannot be attributed to the fact that the particular thematic role is linked to direct object position. German, like English, allows null instantiation of direct objects in cases like (3.62), in which the null complement, while indefinite, is conventionally interpreted as denoting a specific category (Fillmore 1986):

(3.62) Er trinkt wieder.
'He's drinking [alcohol] again.'

Under a construction-based account of argument structure, these facts can be represented in a straightforward way. Each construction defines constraints on null complementation. In the case of the pattern exemplified in (3.60b), we follow Fillmore and Kay (1997) in assuming that null complementation is licensed by the linking construction which pairs a locative argument with an oblique grammatical function. In the case of the *be*-pattern, null instantiation is licensed by the linking construction which pairs a theme argument with oblique as exemplified in (3.61b). (Formal details of this construction will be provided in chapter 4.) The constructional account of null complementation is actually implicit in Brinkmann's original statement of the Deindividuation Hypothesis, presented in section 2.3 as (2.30) and repeated here as (3.63):

(3.63) The direct object of a transitive locative verb may be omitted only when the quantificational properties of the corresponding argument are irrelevant; the argument may then be existentially bound (Brinkmann 1997:113).

Despite the fact that Brinkmann claims to have provided a general constraint governing omissibility of themes, the principle quoted above is not general but particular—it concerns a particular pairing of syntax and semantics which we will describe in chapter 4 as the OBLIQUE-THEME CONSTRUCTION, a construction which unifies with the *be*-pattern.

3.3 Valence Augmentation

As described in section 2.2, an alternation-based account cannot plausibly represent *be*-predications for which no 'source' or 'input' verb exists. One case of this nature is that in which the *be*-pattern 'adds' arguments that were not part of the theta frame of the unprefixed analog. One such case is that of *bemogeln* 'swindle', discussed in section 2.2 with respect to examples (2.18-2.19), repeated here as (3.64-3.65). An attested example illustrating both prefixed and unprefixed uses of *mogeln* in a single passage is given as (3.66):

(3.64) Peter hat beim Kartenspielen **gemogelt**.
'Peter cheated in cards.'

(3.65) Peter hat mich beim Kartenspielen **bemogelt**.
'Peter cheated (lit. *be*-cheated) me in cards.'

(3.66) WKD/bza.00141, Berliner Zeitung/89.12.07/s:3.
W. Schwanitz: Es ist beträchtlich. Prozentzahlen würden das verdeutlichen, die kann ich aber nicht nennen. Kein Geheimdienst dieser Erde tut das oder er **mogelt**. Ich will Sie nicht **bemogeln**.
'W. Schwanitz: It is a considerable number. Percentages would underscore this but I cannot give them. No secret service on earth does that, or they swindle. I don't want to *be*-swindle you.'

In (3.65), as in the last sentence of (3.66), *Ich will Sie nicht bemogeln*, an undergoer argument is added to the theta frame of the input verb. An additional case of valence augmentation was discussed in section 2.3

with respect to example (2.17), repeated here as (3.67):

(3.67) Message ID <35fa4ec9.0@netnews.web.de>
SELBSTKLIMMER = Kletterpflanzen, die mit speziellen Haftorganen Wände oder andere Flächen direkt **bewachsen**, Beispiele: HAFTWURZELN bei Efeu HAFTSCHEIBENRANKEN bei Wildem Wein.
'Self-climbers=climbing plants that directly *be*-grow walls or other surfaces with the help of special adhesive/sticky extremities, for instance, sticky roots in the case of ivy, sticky tendrils in the case of wild vine.'

In (3.67) the object function is linked to an argument whose status is that of an adjunct within the valence frame of the unprefixed verb (*wachsen*). The final case of valence augmentation discussed in 2.3 combines both aspects of valence augmentation displayed by the two classes of examples exemplified by *bemogeln* and *bewachsen*: the direct object represents a participant role which would otherwise have adjunct status and the subject represents a participant role which is not licensed at all by the unprefixed verb. The examples (2.20-2.22) used to exemplify this case for the verbs *regnen* and *beregnen* in section 2.3 are repeated here as (3.68-3.70):

(3.68) *Peter **regnete** die Blumen mit der Gießkanne.
'Peter rained the flowers with the watering can.'

(3.69) *Das Gewitter **regnete** drei Tage lang.
'The thunderstorm rained for three days.'

(3.70) Message ID <6xulta5r4nB@link-m54.link-m.de>
Damals wäre um ein Haar ein Flüssiggastank in Mitleidenschaft gezogen worden [...] die Petershausner Feuerwehr mußte diesen daher intensiv **beregnen**.
'Back then a tank full of liquid gas almost got damaged [...] the Petershausen fire department therefore had to make a great effort to spray water on (lit. *be*-rain) it.'

While, as we showed above, each of these classes proves problematic for an alternation-based view of argument structure, in which rules effect changes in the way in which a given set of argument roles is expressed, these classes receive a straightforward and motivated account under the constructional view. On the constructional account, as described above, the valence set licensed by a linking construction may properly include that licensed by the verb with which that construction combines. Where verb and construction assign identical argument roles, as in the case of the subject argument in (3.67), the two roles simply fuse.[13] Where the semantic scheme associated with the construction assigns a thematic role or roles *not* licensed by the theta frame of the verb, there is override as per the principle in (3.51): the argument roles of the construction are 'added' to the verb's theta frame as verb meaning and construction meaning are combined. What this means in the case of a sentence like (3.67) is that the meaning of the verb *wachsen* is combined with the meaning of the construction via the means relation. The predicate-argument structure resulting from the integration of verb and construction meaning contains a participant which denotes the location covered by means of growth. In chapter 4, we will discuss in detail the mechanism by which appropriate assignments of grammatical functions are made to each argument licensed by the construction.

3.4 Valence Creation

The extreme case of valence augmentation is that in which the head of the *be*-predicate is not a valence-taking element in the lexicon. These are cases of valence creation, as exemplified by deadjectival and denominal *be*-predications. While deadjectival and denominal *be*-verbs are highly prototypical instances of the *be*-pattern, the Brinkmann analysis, as we saw in 2.2 above, is forced to posit phonologically null verbs in their input semantic representations—a move which requires recourse to abstract constructs of dubious validity and the stipulation that the input semantic representation cannot be lexicalized. On the constructional account, valence creation comes about through the same highly general mechanism that underlies valence augmentation. Let us examine again the examples of valence creation (2.13) and (2.15) discussed in section 2.2.2. These examples are repeated here as (3.71) and (3.73), respectively. For each, alternate versions (3.72) and (3.74) are given to illustrate the function of the input lexical item:

(3.71) Message ID <4lq28k$lsr@nz12.rz.uni-karlsruhe.de>
Also *m.E.* regelt 41, wie ein Radweg zu **beschildern** ist und wer darauf was zu suchen hat und wer nicht, und dies unabhängig davon, ob der Radweg neben einer Straße liegt oder durch die Pampa führt.

[13] For fusion to take place, the relevant roles of verb and construction need not always be identical; they may instead by merely compatible, as in the case of *befahren* '*be*-drive', illustrated in (4.85). The bivalent version of the *be*-construction calls for a theme, while the verb *fahren* supplies an agent. However, since this verb denotes directed motion, the agent is also a theme, and therefore fusion of the verb's agent argument and the construction's theme argument is straightforward—the subject denotatum can easily be construed as both agent and theme.

'Well, *in my opinion* [paragraph] 41 regulates how a bike path needs to be equipped with traffic signs (lit. *be*-traffic-signed) and who has any business on it and who doesn't, and it does so independently of whether the bike path runs next to a street or through the middle of the prairie.'

(3.72) Also *m.E.* regelt 41, wie die **Schilder** auf einem Radweg **aufgestellt** werden müssen und wer darauf was zu suchen hat und wer nicht, und dies unabhängig davon, ob der Radweg neben einer Straße liegt oder durch die Pampa führt.
'Well, *in my opinion* [paragraph] 41 regulates how traffic signs have to be put up on a bike path and who has any business on it and who doesn't, and it does so independently of whether the bike path runs next to a street or through the middle of the prairie.'

(3.73) Süddeutsche Zeitung, March 4, 1996
Deutsche Grenzschützer **befreiten** die Geiseln am 18. Oktober 1977 in Mogadischu; Andrawes überlebte als einziger der Terroristen.
'Members of the German border patrol freed (lit. *be*-freed) the hostages on October 18, 1977 in Mogadishu; Andrawes was the only one of the terrorists to survive.'

(3.74) Deutsche Grenzschützer **bekamen** die Geiseln am 18. Oktober 1977 in Mogadischu **frei**; Andrawes überlebte als einziger der Terroristen.
'Members of the German border patrol got the hostages free on October 18, 1977 in Mogadishu; Andrawes was the only one of the terrorists to survive.'

On the constructional account, the valence-creation cases in examples (3.71) and (3.73) are cases of reconciliation which are identical to those discussed in section 3.3, with two important exceptions. First, cases of valence creation involve a form-class override: the nominal or adjectival syntactic feature of the input element is overridden by the verbal syntactic feature of the construction in accordance with (3.51), the override principle. Second, cases of valence creation do not involve fusion of participant roles in input and constructional theta frames, quite simply because the open-class element which combines with the *be*-construction in cases like (3.71) and (3.73) has no theta frame. Instead, the repertoire of roles contributed by the input item are participants in the larger semantic frame which constitutes our understanding of the socio-cultural context in which the property or entity plays a role. By semantic frames we have in mind the schemas Fillmore (1977, 1982, 1985) uses to represent lexical semantics and which underlie his contention that all linguistic meaning is 'relativized to scenes' (1977:59). For example, in (2.13) the nominal *Schild* is meaningful only relative to a schema which includes streets and streetworkers. In (2.15) the adjective *frei* is meaningful only relative to a schema which includes captives and liberators. By combining with the *be*-construction, the noun not only receives a valence structure and concomitant event construal, but also an event construal which is compatible with the semantics of the *be*-construction. In other words, the event denoted by the predication is one involving coverage of a location by a theme. For example, *beschildern* in (2.13) denotes the activity of placing signs at regular intervals along the bike path.

The question that arises here is precisely how we capture the crucial felicity condition identified by Clark and Clark (1979) upon the use of denominal verbs: the source or 'parent' word must denote one thematic role in the situation, while the remaining surface arguments of the denominal denote other roles in that situation. How do we ensure, for example, that the parent noun of the verb *beschildern*, *Schild*, is taken to be the theme of the coverage event? Our solution, which will be implemented in chapter 4, is to reframe this question by rejecting the assumption that the parent nominal in fact fills the theme role. The parent nominal is not referential, and therefore could not be said to refer to any particular participant in any given event. Instead, we claim, the parent nominal renders the actual theme argument RECOVERABLE, and thereby omissible as per the oblique-theme construction, which allows null instantiation of theme arguments as discussed in section 3.2. Evidence for this claim comes from the fact that any theme argument whose identity the interpreter might not readily recover from the category denoted by the parent noun may be present, as in the case of (3.75):

(3.75) 4809664
Die Berkersheimer Grundschule in der Untergasser Hohl wird mit zwei Tafeln **beschildert**, die in der Straßenverkehrsordnung gar nicht vorgesehen sind.
'The Berkersheim Elementary School on Untergasser Hohl Street will be *be*-signed with two signs that are not provided for at all by the traffic regulations.'

A final example of valence creation gives particularly strong evidence in favor of an approach in which both the *be*-pattern and the oblique-goal construction are inherently meaningful. These are examples involving nonce verbs, like that discussed by Wunderlich (1987:304). Wunderlich observes that if the nonexisting verb *prillen* is formed and taken to mean 'hit with a racket' (a meaning that is not otherwise lexicalized in German), the verb can participate in both the oblique-goal construction and the *be*-construction:

(3.76) Sie **prillt** den Ball **auf** die Wand.
'She prills the ball onto the wall.'

(3.77) Sie **beprillt** die Wand mit dem Ball.
'She *be*-prills the wall with the ball.'

In (3.76) and (3.77), we see that it is the skeletal structure of the construction alone, and not any aspect of lexical meaning, that licenses the interpretation of these sentences as involving causation of motion and the particular reading of (3.77) as involving multiple such events. A plausible account of valence creation requires the recognition of both 'bottom up' contributions to meaning (lexical meaning) and 'top down' contributions to meaning (constructional meaning). The interpretation of denominal verbs like *beschildern* involves not only the top-down imposition of valence structure from the construction but the bottom-up importation of the rich frame semantics of the nominal element with which the construction combines.

3.5 Exteriority

The constructional account of the exteriority constraint discussed in section 2.3.3 with respect to the construal of *bewerfen* in (2.38) is straightforward. Rather than appealing to a constraint imposed by the prefix, whose meaning, as discussed in section 2.3.3 would be construction-specific anyway, we view exteriority as a topological semantic type constraint on the theme argument: it must be planar. The claim that this constraint belongs to the construction is substantiated by override effects as described by (3.51). Example (2.38) provides an example of such an override, but perhaps the most cogent example of this phenomenon comes from the verb *befüllen* 'fill'. This verb at first appears to violate the planar surface constraint in that it necessarily describes an effect upon the INTERIOR of a three-dimensional space. However, we notice that attested uses of *befüllen* have iterative readings, as in (3.78-3.79):

(3.78) *Frankfurter Allgemeine Zeitung*, August 7, 1990
Außerdem müßten Betriebe, die Mehrwegflaschen **befüllen**, eine plötzliche Erhöhung ihrer Pfandrückstellungen bewältigen.
'Moreover companies that *be*-fill returnable bottles would have to cope with a sudden increase of their reserve for deposits.'

(3.79) *Süddeutsche Zeitung*, July 25, 1994.
Darüber hinaus werden im Jemen 5 Milliarden US-Dollar für eine Erdgas-Verflüssigungsanlage bei Aden oder Mukalla fällig, um dort die Tanker nach Japan zu **befüllen**.
'Moreover 5 billion US dollars will become due for a natural gas liquefaction plant near Aden or Mukalla that serves to *be*-fill the tankers to Japan.'

In (3.78), the iterative reading comes from a construal in which bottles are repeatedly returned and filled. In (3.79), the iterative reading comes from a construal in which tankers are repeatedly emptied and filled. The iterative reading arises in each case via the override principle (3.51), which requires that the filling scene denoted by the verb be reconciled with the planar coverage scene denoted by the construction. The 'compromise construal' is one in which an exterior surface is affected: the iterated filling events, insofar as each occupies a different pair of coordinates, collectively define a planar region over which coverage is effected. Further discussion of the relation of the exteriority constraint to the various senses of the construction will take place in chapter 5.

3.6 Holism

On the account offered here, the source of the holism constraint is the semantics of the *be*-construction, rather than a general principle concerning the application of predicates to their direct arguments—a principle which we saw in section 2.3.1 not to be a general constraint on predication. We also depart from Pinker's account of the locative alternation, since we do not attribute the affectedness implication of *be*-predications to any general principle governing the construal of direct objects. Instead, we view the holism effect as entailed by the situation type denoted by the *be*-construction. The *be*-construction requires coverage of location by theme at a given point in time or over the course of time.

3.7 Concreteness and Compositionality

The constructional model is based on the sign: constructions are form-meaning pairs which differ from words only in internal complexity. Like Montague Grammar, Construction Grammar pairs surface structure with a semantic representation; no 'deep' level of semantic representation intervenes between these two levels. Thus, the constructional model does not rely on either lexico-semantic 'transformations' or multiple types of semantic representation (like those representations which are input to L-command and functional application in the Brinkmann-Wunderlich model). In addition, the constructional model does not rely upon abstract (phonologically null) elements; denominal verbs, for example, are not represented as arguments of phonologically unrealized verbs but as nominals which assume valence structures by virtue of unification with an argument-structure construction.

The constructional model is concrete, and therefore conforms well to Jackendoff's Grammatical Constraint—a constraint on semantics which, in Jackendoff's words, 'serve(s) to make semantic theory responsible to the facts of grammar' (1983:18). Since syntax encodes propositions related to events and states of affairs, we must assume that it does this in an efficient and relatively transparent way. It therefore makes sense to base syntactic theory on the assumption that argument-structure patterns directly express basic-level scenes. But in attributing meaning to syntactic patterns in the interest of concreteness, we potentially undermine the fundamental purpose of syntactic theory: to describe sentence meaning compositionally. If the conceptual content of a sentence now comes not only from lexical conceptual structures but also from the syntactic patterns that contain those lexical items, we sacrifice a constrained model of semantic composition. Like Jackendoff, we question the assumption that this model must necessarily be preserved. As Jackendoff observes:

> [A] more constrained theory is only as good as the empirical evidence for it. If elevated to the level of dogma (or reduced to the level of presupposition) so that no empirical evidence can be brought to bear on it, then it is not being treated scientifically. (1997a:50)

Jackendoff's response is a reminder that the empirical criteria must take precedence over the theory-internal criterion of parsimony. But we have an additional response, which Jackendoff, an advocate of enriched composition but not of a construction-based syntax, does not give: the constructional model is in fact compositional, although not in the standard sense. If the meaning of a sentence is the result of integration of verbal and constructional semantics in accordance with the override principle of (3.51) then that meaning results from semantic composition. In other words, we do not abandon a constrained theory of sentence meaning by acknowledging the existence of 'top down' or constructional meaning. The mechanism of unification ensures that sentence meaning is the result of a constrained combination of symbolic structures. The next chapter will be devoted to an examination of the formal mechanism of unification as applied to the relevant linking constructions.

4

The Linking Constructions in Combination

As we established in the previous chapter, a linking construction, like a Saussurean sign, relates meaning and form: it specifies a set of semantic roles, related within a schematic scene, and the grammatical realization of one or more of these roles (subject, object, oblique). Crucially, the repertoire of thematic roles licensed by the linking construction may include thematic roles which are not in the valence sets of verbs which can combine with that linking construction. The concept of 'alternation', i.e., variable argument-structure, is represented by the existence of two or more complementary linking possibilities for a single verb. Complementarity is ensured by the inability of two conflicting linking patterns to unify, since each places incompatible specifications on a given verb entry. For example, a theme argument cannot be linked to both subject and object functions. Compatible linking patterns will, however, be simultaneously applicable. Among these are the transitive and oblique-goal patterns. A sentence is grammatical insofar as it is licensed by a unified combination of constructions. It is ungrammatical insofar as it is not licensed by any unified combination of constructions.

Let us begin our exploration of linking patterns and their methods of combination by establishing a few basic facts about linking in *be*-predications, both trivalent and bivalent. We will begin with some observations about the alternations shown in examples (4.80-4.83):

(4.80) MK1/LSO.00000, Strittmatter, Ole Bienkopp
Er fährt bis auf Sernos Hof und **lädt** seine Koffer **auf** einen Pferdewagen. Das Auto wird in die Scheune geschoben .
'He drives up to Serno's farm and loads his suitcases onto a horse-drawn carriage. The car gets pushed into the barn.'

(4.81) Er fährt bis auf Sernos Hof und **belädt** einen Pferdewagen mit seinen Koffern.
'He drives up to Serno's farm and loads (lit. *be*-loads) a horse-drawn carriage with his suitcases.'

(4.82) Nebenan befand sich Olga Gorenkamps Nähzimmer, die Tür war nur angelehnt. Jetzt **sprachen** sie eingehend **über** die neue Situation. Und sie war äußerst günstig für das Weingut.
'Next door was Olga Gorenkamp's sewing room. The door was ajar. Now they were talking about the new situation thoroughly. And it was extremely favorable for the winery.'

(4.83) R1/TL1.09008 de Groot, B.: Dein Vater wird uns liebgewinnen.
Nebenan befand sich Olga Gorenkamps Nähzimmer, die Tür war nur angelehnt. Jetzt **besprachen** sie eingehend die neue Situation. Und sie war äußerst günstig für das Weingut.
'Next door was Olga Gorenkamp's sewing room. The door was ajar. Now they were discussing (lit. *be*-speaking) the new situation thoroughly. And it was extremely favorable for the winery.'

One can make the following general observations about the linking alternations shown in (4.80-4.83). First, the complements of the spatial prepositions in the non-*be*-sentences correspond to the accusative direct objects of the *be*-sentences. In example (4.80) above, *Pferdewagen* 'horse-drawn carriage' is the complement of the preposition *auf* 'onto', but in sentence (4.81) it is the direct object of *beladen* 'load [a surface]'. Second, the prepositional phrases headed by *mit* 'with' in the *be*-sentences are omissible. Thus, one could omit the prepositional phrase *mit seinen Koffern* in (4.81) but one could not omit the corresponding nonoblique, *seine Koffer*, in (4.80). Third, active *be*-sentences always have a direct object (as in (4.81) and (4.83)), whether or not the corresponding *be*-less sentences are transitive (as in (4.80)) or intransitive (as in (4.82)). In all active-form *be*-sentences, the direct object represents the thematic role of LOCATIVE. In trivalent *be*-predications like (4.81), the subject represents the thematic role of AGENT. The agent is that participant responsible for effecting contact between the location and a THEME argument. The theme argument may be expressed by an oblique, as in (4.81) (*mit seinen Koffern*), or it may instead be evoked by the semantics of a denominal verb as in (4.84):

(4.84) MK1/LGB.00000, Grass, Die Blechtrommel, Roman.
Der alte Heilandt weigerte sich, den Tafelwagen bis zu den Städtischen Friedhöfen zu ziehen. Er habe noch Stiefel zu **besohlen**, sagte er, und müsse es kurz machen.
'Old Heilandt refused to pull the cart as far as the Municipal Cemetery. He said he still had to put soles on (lit. *be*-sole) some boots and had to hurry.'

In (4.84), the theme is the sole, which is transferred to the location denoted by the nominal object *Stiefel* 'boots'. Examples like (4.84) show that, under specific circumstances, a *be*-predication can denote transfer in the absence of an overtly coded theme argument. We propose that the semantic requirements of the *be*-construction include a theme argument, and that in the case of denominal verbs like *besohlen*, that theme argument will be syntactically unrealized under the same conditions of recoverability that we find in the case of non-denominal transfer verbs like *beladen*. In bivalent *be*-predications like (4.85) below, the theme argument is linked to subject position. In examples like (4.85), the subject denotes a self-propelled or agentive theme:

(4.85) MK1/MHE.00000, Heuss, Erinnerungen 1905-1933, Memoiren.
Nun hatte ich wohl die Ostsee **befahren** und die Nordsee geschmeckt, aber das 'Schwäbische Meer', wie man in meiner Jugend den Bodensee nannte—die Formel ist verdorrt—,war mir fremd geblieben.
'True, I had sailed (lit. *be*-driven) the Baltic Sea and had a taste of the North Sea, but the "Swabian Sea", as people called the Bodensee in my youth—the phrase has withered away since—had remained unfamiliar to me.'

As transitives, all verbs prefixed by *be*- are compatible with a passive linking, in which the locative argument appears in subject position, and the argument which would be realized as the subject in an active clause is an oblique or is not expressed at all. Passive *be*-predications are exemplified in sentences (4.86-4.87) below:

(4.86) Message ID <199701181227.a2507@lu.maus.de>
In dem unter israelischer Kontrolle verbleibendem Viertel Hebrons gab es am Vormittag Unruhen. Sicherheitskräfte wurden mit Steinen **beworfen**.
'In the morning there were riots in the quarter of Hebron that is going to remain under Israeli control. Security forces were pelted (lit. *be*-thrown) with stones.'

(4.87) Message ID <01bc018bd8bd55609d05bac3@familie-beco>
Selbst bei längeren Schlechtwetterperioden fühlt man sich nicht eingeengt und dank der Koch- und Heizmöglichkeit (offenes Lagerfeuer in der Mitte) kann ein Tipi bei jedem Wetter problemlos **bewohnt** werden.
'Even during an extended period of bad weather one does not feel confined, and due to the possibility of cooking and heating (open campfire in the middle), a teepee can be inhabited (lit. *be*-lived) in any kind of weather without a problem.'

In (4.86), a trivalent verb is combined with a passive linking construction, whereby the locative participant is linked to subject position, the theme is coded by an oblique, and the agent is unrealized. In (4.87), a bivalent verb is unified with the passive linking construction. The locative is again linked to subject position, while the theme is unrealized.

We can account for all of the linking patterns in which *be*-verbs appear by assuming five linking constructions: the *be*-construction itself, the TRANSITIVE construction, the PASSIVE construction, the SUBJECT construction and the OBLIQUE-THEME construction. All of the linking constructions which we will discuss in this chapter, with the exception of the *be*-construction itself, were originally postulated by Fillmore and Kay (1997: ch.8). However, for those constructions which denote situation types, we will augment the Fillmore and Kay representations with the formalism developed by Goldberg (1995) for representing the interaction between constructional and verb semantics. The mechanism which ensures the appropriate interaction between linking constructions is UNIFICATION, as described by Fillmore and Kay (1997) and Kay and Fillmore (1999). Unification of constructions can best be described in terms of a metaphor involving the superimposition of slides. Any slide (construction) can be superimposed upon any other as long as the semantic and syntactic specifications on each slide 'show through'—that is, provided there is no conflict among the specifications on the slides in the stack. We will depart from the Fillmore and Kay account of argument-structure unification only in one regard: we will allow the override of the syntactic form class of an open-class element for cases in which nouns and adjectives unify with the *be*-construction, a verb-headed construction. This move seems to be the only way that we can capture the observed form-class fluidity without resorting to the assumption of radical and unconstrained polysemy which was criticized in section 3.1.

All linking constructions operate upon the valence set specified by a given lexical item. The number of valence elements specified by a given linking construction may be greater or less than the number of valence elements specified by the lexical verb. The only requirement involved in unification of verbs and linking constructions is that all thematic roles included in the valence set of the verb and the linking construction(s) must be syntactically realized.[14] One can think of the linking constructions as being superimposed upon (or stacked on top of) a given verb's lexical entry (although in reality the interacting constructions apply simultaneously). The lexical entry contains a minimal valence, i.e., an array of thematic roles, whose grammatical expression is determined by the linking construction or constructions applied. A minimal lexical entry which is unified with linking constructions is said to be a FULLY SPECIFIED lexical entry: one in which every thematic role supplied by the lexical entry is linked with a grammatical function.

Let us now examine the individual linking constructions, and the way in which they interact to license *be*-predications. The TRANSITIVE CONSTRUCTION is given in Figure 3. The SYNTACTIC attribute of the

$$\begin{bmatrix} \text{syn} & \begin{bmatrix} \text{cat} & \text{v} \\ \text{voice} & \text{active} \end{bmatrix} \\ \text{sem} & \begin{bmatrix} \ldots \end{bmatrix} \\ \text{val} & \left\{ \text{role} \begin{bmatrix} \text{gf} & \text{obj} \\ \theta & \text{DA-} \end{bmatrix} \right\} \end{bmatrix}$$

FIGURE 3 The Transitive Construction

Transitive construction has the value of lexical verb; that is, the elements whose linking is determined by the Transitive construction are verbs. The VALENCE attribute of the construction has as its value a set of elements. Each of the valence members specified has a ROLE attribute. The role attribute has as its value the grammatical function (gf) and thematic role (θ) of the particular valence member (i.e., argument).[15] In Figure 3, the abbreviation DA, which appears as the value of the theta-role attribute, stands for DISTINGUISHED ARGUMENT. The distinguished argument is that argument which has the greatest number of agentive properties, with respect to the other participant roles in the frame evoked by the verb (cf. Dowty 1991, Fillmore and Kay 1997, Foley and Van Valin

[14]This constraint, referred to by Fillmore and Kay (1997: ch 2) as the Constraint on Semantic Coherence, is strongly reminiscent of the Theta Criterion in Government and Binding theory.

[15]For ease of exposition, we will not include the ROLE attribute unless BOTH a grammatical function and thematic role are specified for a given valence member.

1984). In Figure 3, DA is a binary feature. We assume, in accordance with Fillmore and Kay (1997:29), that the lexical entry of the verb will specify which argument within its theta frame is the DA; all arguments other than the DA will be marked DA- in the lexical entry. As shown in Figure 3, the transitive linking construction provides only that an argument which is not the DA is linked to the grammatical function of OBJECT. The SEMANTIC attribute of the transitive construction has an unspecified value ([. . .]). Following Goldberg (1995:118-119), we presume that the transitive linking construction is associated with a prototype-based semantic model whose core involves a volitional actor effecting a change in another participant. We use the unspecified *sem* value to index the model which Goldberg describes.

The Transitive construction says nothing about the linking of subject. How then do we ensure that the role of subject is linked to the DA in an active clause? The answer to this question is not obvious, since the SUBJECT CONSTRUCTION, shown in Figure 4, provides only that every lexical entry assigns the grammatical function SUBJECT. It does not require that a *particular* thematic role be linked to subject. However, in a bivalent active clause, like (4.85), the interaction of the

$$\begin{bmatrix} \text{syn} & \begin{bmatrix} \text{cat} & \text{V} \begin{bmatrix} \text{lex} & + \end{bmatrix} \end{bmatrix} \\ \text{val} & \left\{ \begin{bmatrix} \text{gf} & \text{subj} \end{bmatrix} \right\} \end{bmatrix}$$

FIGURE 4 The Subject Construction

Transitive and Subject constructions will ensure that the DA is linked to subject position: the Transitive construction requires that the argument marked DA- (the location) is linked to object position, while the argument marked DA+ (the theme) will be linked *by default* to subject position. Why should the linking of theme and subject occur by default? In other words, why shouldn't the subject construction specify that the subject role is linked to the thematic role marked DA+? Such an approach would be consistent with linking accounts based upon an accessibility or thematic-role hierarchy. The rationale behind the default linking of subject is provided by the analysis of passive constructions.

In a passive construction, it is not the distinguished argument which is linked to subject position, but an argument which is not the DA. The Passive construction, shown in Figure 5, does not specify which thematic role will be linked to the subject function. The Passive construction says

$$\begin{bmatrix} \text{syn} & \begin{bmatrix} \text{cat} & \text{V} \\ \text{form} & \text{PastPart} \end{bmatrix} \\ \text{val} & \left\{ \begin{bmatrix} \text{role} & \begin{bmatrix} \text{gf} & \text{obl} \\ \text{DA} & + \end{bmatrix} \\ \text{syn} & \text{P}\big[\textit{von}\big]/\text{zero} \end{bmatrix} \right\} \end{bmatrix}$$

FIGURE 5 The Passive Construction

only that the DA will be linked to the grammatical function OBLIQUE, where the oblique role may be realized either as a prepositional phrase headed by *von* 'by' or as a null complement. While the potential for null complementation is explicitly licensed by the Passive linking construction, the exploitation of this possibility will be subject to the general Gricean conditions of omission up to recoverability (Horn 1984). For a passive sentence involving a bivalent verb like *bewohnen* in (4.87), the interaction of the Passive and Subject constructions is as follows: the Passive construction links the DA (the theme) to the oblique grammatical function (whose realization in this case is null), while the Subject construction links the locative argument (*ein Tipi*) to the subject grammatical function.[16]

We have now discussed the interaction of the Transitive and Subject constructions, on the one hand, and the interaction of the Passive and Subject constructions, on the other. However, we have limited our discussion to bivalent *be*-predications. We will now proceed to discuss the linking properties of trivalent *be*-predications. In the course of this discussion, we will answer a question raised by the CG formulation of the Transitive linking construction: Why does this construction not specify, in accordance with Goldberg's formulation of the Transitive construction (1995:118-119), that the thematic role of the object is that of PROTO-PATIENT (in terms of Dowty 1991)? The analysis of trivalent *be*-

[16]We have said nothing about the situation type denoted by the Passive construction. Rather than denoting a particular situation type, the Passive linking construction receives its Aktionsart value from the Aktionsart of the verb with which it combines. This Aktionsart value must unify with that of the passive auxiliary *be*, which likewise bears no independent Aktionsart value. In English, we have direct evidence for this type of aspectual feature transmission. The combination of Passive with a perfective verb like *question* is perfective, as evidenced by the felicity of the progressivized passive *They were being questioned.* The combination of Passive with an imperfective verb like *prefer* is imperfective, as evidenced by the peculiarity (without supporting context) of the progressivized passive *?White wine is being preferred by most Americans.*

predications involves the OBLIQUE-THEME construction, which is given in Figure 6.

$$\left[\begin{array}{ll} \text{syn} & \left[\text{cat} \quad \text{V}\right] \\ \text{sem} & \textsc{cause-cover}<\textsc{agent}, \textsc{theme}, \textsc{location}> \\ \text{val} & \left\{\left[\theta \quad \text{agt}\right], \left[\theta \quad \text{location}\right], \left[\begin{array}{ll} \text{role} & \left[\begin{array}{ll} \text{gf} & \text{obl} \\ \theta & \text{theme} \end{array}\right] \\ \text{syn} & \text{P}\left[\textit{mit}\right]/\text{zero} \end{array}\right]\right\} \end{array}\right]$$

FIGURE 6 The Oblique-Theme Construction

This construction has as its semantic value an event type in which an agent causes a theme to cover a location (the goal).[17] Although we have not shown the relevant unification indices, the agent, theme and goal of this event type will unify with those same thematic roles in the valence set of the lexical verb. The event type denoted by the Oblique-Theme construction is identical to that denoted by the trivalent applicative construction, ensuring unification between the two constructions. The only linking constraint imposed by the Oblique-Theme construction is this: the theme argument links to the oblique grammatical function, which is realized either as a prepositional phrase headed by *mit* or as a null (pragmatically recoverable) complement.

We have said nothing in the statement of the Oblique-Theme construction about the construal of the theme as nonindividuated. We have chosen to remain agnostic concerning the appropriate representation of the nonindividuated construal, since it is a potential rather than a requirement. As Brinkmann and others have observed, an individuated construal of the theme is compatible with applicative semantics, as in *Erna bekochte zehn Männer mit einem einzigen Truthahn* 'Erna *be*-cooked ten men with a single turkey'. The Oblique-Theme construction unifies with denominal applicative verbs like *besohlen*, as in (4.84). Here, the identity of the theme argument can be reconstructed on the basis of the semantics of the lexical form with which the various linking constructions unify. This lexical form is a nominal; it is only by virtue of unifying with an argument-structure construction—in this case the trivalent applicative construction—that the nominal receives a theta frame.

[17] We have not specified the Aktionsart class of this event type because as we will see in Chapter 5, the Applicative Construction does not specify telicity of the transfer event.

In accordance with the Gricean principle of omission up to recoverability (modulo constructional constraints), a theme argument which is not recoverable from the type denoted by the verb, owing to the greater specificity of that theme argument, will be syntactically realized, as in the English example *He soled my shoes with gum soles* and the German example given in (3.75).

Let us now see how the Oblique-Theme construction interacts with the Transitive, Subject, and Passive constructions to license both passive and active trivalent *be*-predications. In the case of (4.81), *Er belädt einen Pferdewagen mit seinen Koffern* 'He *be*-loads a horse-drawn carriage with his suitcases', the Transitive, Subject and Oblique-Theme constructions are combined. The Transitive construction links an argument marked DA- to object position. There are two arguments marked DA-, the locative and theme. How does the Transitive construction determine which is linked to the object role? Quite simply, it must be the locative argument which links to the object role, since if the Transitive construction were to link the theme argument with the object role, there would be a failure of unification: the theme argument will also be linked with the OBLIQUE grammatical function, by means of the Oblique-Theme construction. By the same token, the linking of subject to the agent role is the only linking which will not result in a failure of unification, since the theme and locative arguments are assigned oblique and object roles, respectively.

At this point, the alert reader will have noticed that we have failed to provide a linking construction which is needed to license trivalent predications like (4.80), *Er lädt seine Koffer auf einen Pferdewagen*, in which the theme (*seine Koffer*) is linked to the object role and the location (*einen Pferdewagen*) to the oblique role. Sentences of this type require the postulation of an additional linking construction, also discussed by Fillmore and Kay: the Oblique-Goal construction.[18] The Oblique-Goal construction has a semantic value similar to that of the Oblique-Theme construction, but it imposes a distinct linking pattern: while agent and theme roles are unlinked, the GOAL is linked to the oblique grammatical function.

As in the case of (4.81), the Transitive construction will impose a linking by default: this time the THEME is the only otherwise unlinked argument which is marked DA-, and it will therefore be linked to the object role. The Transitive construction licenses both (4.80) and (4.81). It is compatible with both the Oblique-Theme construction and the Oblique-

[18]We have chosen not to display the Oblique-Goal construction simply because it is not relevant to the licensing of *be*-predications.

Goal construction. In positing a default linking of a non-distinguished argument to object position, we achieve this compatibility without creating circularity. If, however, we were to embrace an account of the Transitive Construction in which the object role is linked with the Proto-Patient role, we would not be able to avoid circularity. Such an account would force us to regard the theme of (4.80) as Proto-Patient and the Goal of (4.81) as Proto-Patient, simply based upon the assignment of object status. If a Proto-Patient is diagnosed as such because of its object status, and an object is analyzed as a Proto-Patient, one concept is defined in terms of the other. We thus prefer to dispense with the Proto-Patient role and embrace default linking to object position in our formulation of the Transitive Construction.

Since the Subject construction also imposes a default linking, it can, in concert with the Passive and Oblique-Theme constructions, license passive trivalent *be*-predications like (4.86), *Sicherheitskräfte wurden mit Steinen beworfen.* The Passive construction links the agent argument to an oblique grammatical function (which receives a null realization), the Oblique-Theme construction links the goal with oblique role, and the Subject construction links the only otherwise unlinked argument (the goal) with the subject role.

The final construction with which we will concern ourselves is the *be*-construction itself. This construction, like the others we have looked at, imposes only a single linking constraint—on the locative thematic role. The grammatical realization of the remaining thematic role or roles will be determined by those constructions with which the *be*-construction combines, including the passive, active, subject and oblique-theme constructions. Figure 7 shows the bivalent version of the *be*-construction. Figure 8 shows the trivalent version.[19] The predicate-argument structures given as values of the *sem* attribute in each of the two figures each displays a distinct degree of aspectual neutrality. In Figure 7, the predicate COVER expresses a situation type which is neutral as to stativity. In Figure 8, the predicate CAUSE-COVER expresses a situation type which, although perfective, is neutral with regard to telicity. Accordingly, as we will see in chapter 5, the coverage implication is compatible with stative, processual (activity) and accomplishment construals.

We postulate that the two versions of the Applicative construction are related via an INHERITANCE LINK. Inheritance networks, as per Lakoff (1987), Goldberg (1995), Michaelis and Lambrecht (1996), and

[19]A more extensive representation of the constructions in Figures 7 and 8 would show the unification requirement between elements in the event structure denoted by the construction and elements in the valence set of the construction. We have avoided showing unification indices in order to simplify the diagrams to the extent possible.

$$\begin{bmatrix} \text{syn} & \begin{bmatrix}\text{cat} & \text{V}\\ \text{form} & \text{Be-prefix}\end{bmatrix} \\ \text{sem} & \begin{bmatrix}\text{COVER<THEME, LOCATION>}\end{bmatrix} \\ \text{PRED<>} & \\ \text{val} & \left\{ \begin{bmatrix}\text{role} & \text{theme}\end{bmatrix}, \begin{bmatrix}\text{sem} & \text{planar region}\\ \text{role} & \begin{bmatrix}\text{gf} & \text{obl-}\\ \theta & \text{location}\end{bmatrix}\end{bmatrix}\right\} \end{bmatrix}$$

FIGURE 7 The bivalent Applicative Construction

$$\begin{bmatrix} \text{syn} & \begin{bmatrix}\text{cat} & \text{V}\\ \text{form} & \text{Be-prefix}\end{bmatrix} \\ \text{sem} & \begin{bmatrix}\text{CAUSE-COVER<AGENT, THEME, LOCATION>}\end{bmatrix} \\ \text{PRED<>} & \\ \text{val} & \left\{ \begin{bmatrix}\text{role} & \text{agent}\end{bmatrix}, \begin{bmatrix}\text{role} & \text{theme}\end{bmatrix}, \begin{bmatrix}\text{sem} & \text{planar region}\\ \text{role} & \begin{bmatrix}\text{gf} & \text{obl-}\\ \theta & \text{location}\end{bmatrix}\end{bmatrix}\right\} \end{bmatrix}$$

FIGURE 8 The trivalent Applicative Construction

Jackendoff (1997b) are used to capture relationships between linguistic signs when these relationships are not sufficiently productive to be represented as rules, but are nevertheless entrenched connections within an associative memory. The inheritance model is similar to that described by Pinker and Prince (1991:232) as the connectionist model of memory. This model is both associative and superpositional: 'individual [linguistic] items are dissolved into sets of features, and similar items [...] overlap in their physical representationsm, sharing representation real estate'. In accordance with the CG tradition as established by Lakoff and Goldberg, among others, we will represent these overlap relations in terms of links in a hierarchical network, where a dominated construction inherits all nonconflicting specifications from the dominating construction. In the case of the two versions of the Applicative construction, we propose that the bivalent version is related to the trivalent version by means of what Goldberg (1995) and Michaelis and Lambrecht (1996) call a SUBPART LINK: the trivalent construction subsumes the semantic representation and syntactic (linking) constraints of the bivalent construction.

Our model of the interaction between a verb and a given version of the Applicative construction, bivalent or trivalent, relies upon the asymmetric manner in which verbs and constructions adhere to Semantic Coherence. Verbs rely on linking constructions in ways that linking constructions do not rely on verbs. The verb adheres to Semantic Coherence by ensuring syntactic expression of each of its arguments through fusion: each role licensed by the verb must fuse with a role licensed by a linking construction. The construction adheres to Semantic Coherence by ensuring syntactic expression of each of its arguments, whether or not each argument is fused with an argument licensed by the verb. This means that the construction's arguments may be expressed by maximal categories (e.g., NP) that are not subcategorized for by the verb.

For the bivalent construction, this situation is exemplified by predications containing *bemogeln* 'cheat': the 'malefactee' argument is added by the construction in Figure 7. This construction also constrains the grammatical function that can be assigned to this role: it must be either subject or object (to be determined by which voice construction, Passive or Active, unifies with this one). For the trivalent construction, verbal-valence augmentation is exemplified by the verb *bebauen* 'build up'. As a creation verb, *bauen* licenses agent and theme arguments. The construction both adds a goal (location) argument to the verbal valence set and restricts the grammatical function to which the location argument can be linked, as described above.[20] Whenever the valence set licensed by

[20]How do we ensure that each verb unifies with the appropriate version of the Applicative construction? As it stands, there is nothing to prevent a trivalent verb like *laden* 'load' from unifying with the bivalent version of the construction. Although the agent of *laden* would not fuse with any role in the theta frame of the bivalent Applicative construction, it would be linked to the SUBJECT grammatical function by the default Subject Principle, since the theme and location are each subject to more specific linkings—Oblique Theme and Applicative, respectively. We also have no obvious way to prevent a bivalent verb like *wandern* 'wander' from unifying with the causative (trivalent) version of the construction. In such an instance, the Applicative would merely contribute an agent to the verb's valence and require nonoblique expression of the location. The theme would be subject to the Oblique Theme linking, and the agent would again receive subject coding due to the Subject Principle. By allowing such unification, we overgenerate, since *bewandern*, e.g., could not be used to denote causation of coverage. It appears that we must stipulate an optimization principle whereby the verb unifies with that version of the Applicative whose valency is closest to its own. However, since the constructional model of partial productivity to be discussed in section 5.5 associates verb classes with constructions, we have an independently motivated mechanism by which to index verbs or verb classes to the appropriate version of the Applicative construction.

the construction properly includes that licensed by the verb, the verb bears a means relation to the event type denoted by the construction.

The PRED variable in Figures 7-8 is used in accordance with Goldberg (1995) to represent the open-class element with which the construction unifies. The angled brackets to the right of the PRED variable represent the theta frame licensed by the open-class element. As described in section 3.4, the open-class element with which the *be*-construction unifies may be an inherently non-relational element, and thereby lack argument structure. For example, the open-class element may be a noun, as in the case of *beschildern* 'put up traffic signs' and *besohlen* 'sole'. As we argued in that section, appropriate thematic elements can be found in the rich background knowledge with which the particular word is associated. This semantic frame contains participant roles, and these are the roles which will be 'plugged into' the argument set associated with the filler of the PRED variable. In the case of the verb *besohlen*, for example, this set will contain the cobbler, the sole and the shoe. These frame-specific roles are required to fuse with the more schematic argument roles licensed by the *be*-construction. For this reason, we assume that denominal verbs necessarily have an elaboration relationship to the applicative construction.

In the next chapter we will show that the semantics of coverage associated with the applicative pattern in its bivalent and trivalent versions is subject to a number of metaphoric and pragmatic extensions.

5

The Semantics of the Applicative Pattern

Like Brinkmann, we argue that *be*-verbs form a coherent semantic category. However, under our account this semantic coherence does not arise from the interaction of syntactic and general pragmatic principles. Rather it is seen as a reflection of the polysemy structure associated with the applicative pattern flagged by the prefix *be*-. In accordance with Goldberg's (1995) analysis of the English ditransitive and other argument-structure patterns, we postulate that the meanings of the *be*-pattern are related via independently motivated patterns of semantic extension, and represent a radial category of senses. As in Lakoff's (1987) description of radial-category structure in classifier systems, the polysemy structure at issue here allows for the cancellation of implications associated with the central sense. We will see that certain senses invoke components of the coverage scenario, like transfer, without entailing coverage.

The exposition of senses associated with the applicative pattern will focus upon specific (and in many cases partially overlapping) classes of verbs (e.g., verbs denoting iterated activity). A question that arises is how this mode of description can be reconciled with our central contention—that the semantic effects which distinguish *be*-predications from their paraphrases are attributable to the semantics of the applicative pattern rather than to the semantics of a particular set of verbs. In other words, if we view the meanings of *be*-predications as the products of a reconciliation procedure whereby the meaning of the verb is brought into conformity with the meaning of the construction, how can we also treat the *be*-verbs as 'stored', i.e., listed, elements? The answer to this question requires us to reject a principle which Langacker (1987) has called the RULE-LIST FALLACY. Langacker applies this term to the (typically implicit) principle which holds that complex structures that can be modeled by an on-line process cannot also be viewed as stored. In a broader sense, certain work on Gricean inference (Morgan 1978, Hinkelman and Allen 1989) can be viewed as undermining the rule-list distinction: while Gricean inferences are readily modeled as algorithms, certain Gricean inferences, in particular those associated with indirect speech acts, may conventionally attach to certain forms (a phenomenon which Morgan refers to as 'short-circuited' conversational implicature). With regard to morphology in particular, Bybee (1995) rejects the idea that the products of regular morphology are exclusively generated online. On the basis of experimental work by Losiewicz (1992), Bybee argues that high-frequency regular past-tense forms are stored in the lexicon. By the same token, we view high-frequency *be*-verbs as clustering in narrowly defined lexical classes that reflect the (conventionalized) patterns of semantic extension observed for the applicative construction. However, we simultaneously maintain that the interpretation of *be*-predications involves the integration of constructional meaning and verb meaning. Were this not so, productive uses of the applicative pattern could not plausibly be modeled (see section 3.4 for argumentation on this point).

The discussion will proceed as follows. In section 5.1., the central sense will be described. In section 5.2., we will describe three classes of *be*-predications which involve metaphorical extensions of this basic meaning. In section 5.3., we will look at five classes of *be*-predications whose meanings relate to the central sense via various inductive inferences. In section 5.4, we will consider the relationship of this semantic analysis to a diachronic analysis of the *be*-pattern given by Ruppenhofer (1999). In particular, we will consider the relationship between the meaning of the *be*-pattern as we have described it and earlier uses of the *be*-prefix to denote CONTAINMENT and PROXIMITY. In section 5.5., we will relate the associative network of senses of the applicative pattern to the phenomenon of partial productivity as described by Pinker (1989) and Goldberg (1995). Finally, in section 5.6., we will discuss the problem of restricting verb-construction interactions, i.e., of accounting for the restrictions on *be*-prefixation discussed by Brinkmann (1997: ch. 6).

This exposition of the usages of the applicative pattern requires a disclaimer: the order of presentation of the verb classes (that is, the usages of the construction) is not intended to reflect any avenue of development of these senses. Instead, we view each sense extension as exploiting a semantic potential inherent in the semantic schema which represents the core sense; no extended sense is viewed as dependent on any other. While there is evidence (to be discussed in section 5.5.) which suggests the historical primacy of the coverage sense of the pattern, we lack the evidence which one would need to provide a relative chronology of the extended senses. Further, we do not intend to suggest that metaphorical extensions of the applicative pattern are recent innovations. Metaphorical extensions, like the use of the applicative pattern to describe thorough discussion of a topic, are old. This particular semantic extension seems to be at least as old as Middle High German, as suggested by a look at the entries for *bereden* 'discuss', *besprechen* 'discuss', *beklagen* 'complain, mourn', *beschreiben* 'describe', *besingen* 'sing about, of', and *bedenken* 'think about, reflect on' in Lexer's (1872) Middle High German dictionary and in the available installments of the Early Modern High German dictionary (Göbel and Reichmann 1999).[21] The radial model of senses which we will offer, in which each sense of the pattern overlaps semantically with the core sense, is consistent with the diachronic facts and provides a plausible model of what might make the various senses cohere synchronically. Figure 9 shows the associative network of meanings which will be discussed in the forthcoming subsections.

5.1 The Prototype

The conceptual archetype with which the applicative pattern is associated is a scene in which a THEME COVERS A SURFACE.[22] This scene is denoted by bivalent verbs like *befahren* in (5.88) and entailed by trivalent verbs like *beschmieren* in (5.89):

(5.88) MK1/MHE.00000, Heuss, Erinnerungen 1905-1933, Memoiren
Nun hatte ich wohl die Ostsee **befahren** und die Nordsee geschmeckt, aber das 'Schwäbische Meer', wie man in meiner Jugend den Bodensee nannte—die Formel ist verdorrt—, war mir fremd geblieben.
'True, I had sailed around (lit. *be*-driven) the Baltic Sea and I had had a taste of the North Sea, but the "Swabian Sea", as people called the Bodensee in my youth—the phrase has withered away since—had remained unfamiliar to me.' (= (4.85)

[21] Within the class of *be*-verbs denoting thorough discussion, there are, however, relatively recent additions. For example, *besprechen* 'discuss' seems to have lacked the 'discuss' sense in Middle High German but meant only '1. agree on 2. talk to, address 3. accuse of 4. consult, confer [used with reciprocal sich]'.

[22] The analysis presented here does not extend to what we may call pseudo-*be*-participles, i.e., to forms that look like participles of *be*-verbs but do in fact not have any related inflected forms. For instance, for *beamtet* 'being state appointed [e.g. as a teacher, judge, etc.]' there is no corresponding verb **beamten*. These ornative applicative participles are analogous to uses of the English past participle to convey attributes, e.g., *long-haired*. See Langacker 1991 for a discussion of the semantic relationship between this use of the past particple and others.

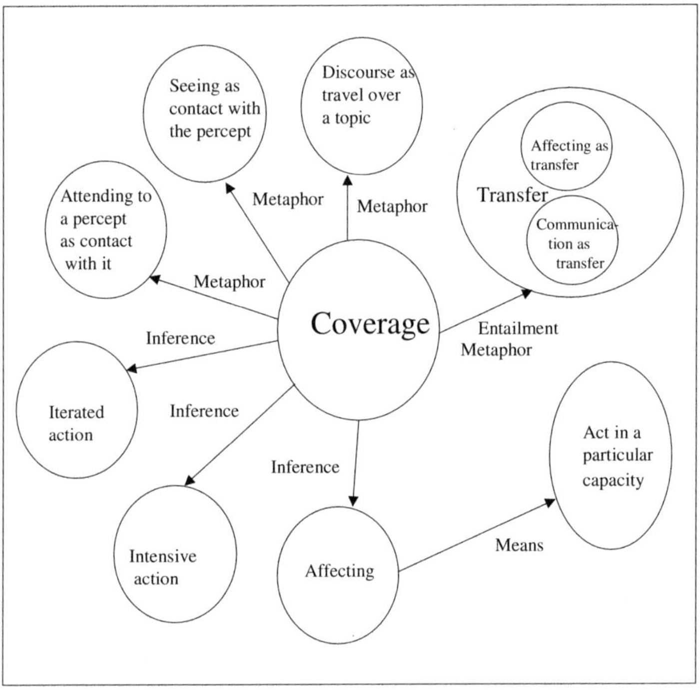

FIGURE 9 The meanings of the applicative pattern

(5.89) 36713673
Jugendliche Straftäter würden bewußt Sitze zerstören, Fenster heraustreten, Wandverkleidungen **beschmieren** oder von den Wänden reißen
'Youth offenders would purposely destroy seats, kick out windows, smear (lit. *be*-smear) wall coverings or tear them off the walls.'

Sentence (5.89) entails that significant portions of each wall hanging are smeared while (5.88) describes extensive travel over the Baltic Sea. However, the notion of saturation at stake here does not require that an entire surface is covered: some parts of each wall hanging may have been spared and areas of the Baltic Sea may not have been reached. Moreover, while the location may often be affected in the sense that it undergoes a noticeable change of state, this is not a necessary consequence of saturation: the Baltic Sea is not changed by the sailor's travels in (5.88).

Finally, notice that saturation may be summed over time, since, for example, the sailor can only occupy a single location at any given time. The type of construal is equivalent to SUMMARY SCANNING, a mode of cognitive processing in which co-activation of scanning events produces a coherent gestalt (Langacker 1987:144-45). In the case of the sailing activity the individual scanning events establish distinctness of sailor and water surface and track the change in relative position. If all the scanning events are overlaid at once (in the way transparencies can be overlaid), there will be only one water surface but many positions occupied by the sailor. This overlay configuration is identical to the coverage schema denoted or entailed by the Applicative construction in its bivalent and trivalent versions.

Notice that while we have used the terms *configuration*, *schema*, *scene* and *archetype* in this section to describe the saturation constraint, we have not referred to an event type. This may appear puzzling, since the constructional model of argument structure upon which we base this analysis is one in which argument-structure patterns denote basic-level event structures. We have avoided the term EVENT STRUCTURE or EVENT TYPE here because these terms suggest that the coverage schema can be characterized as belonging to a particular aspectual class. Coverage is a topological notion, and has no temporal dimension. Accordingly, the saturation constraint may be satisfied by both perfective and imperfective predications.[23] In (5.90), for example, a *be*-predication containing the stative verb *bewohnen* 'inhabit' denotes a situation of coverage which holds at a single point in time:

(5.90) MMM/102.37001: Mannheimer Morgen, 09.02.1991, Leserbriefe
Die alteingesessenen Altriper, die den Ortskern bis jetzt noch **bewohnen**, werden sich eben mit dem noch stärker werdenden Durchgangsverkehr abfinden müssen.
'The long-time Altriperians who up until now are still living in (lit. *be*-living) the town center will just have to get used to the increasing through traffic.'

The coverage concept associated with *bewohnen* is also compatible with a habitual construal, in which a single inhabitant effects coverage of a given location over time (5.91a). As shown in (5.91b), a *bewohnen* predication is anomalous when the location (in this case, a city) is too large to allow an individual to effect coverage over time; the prepositional

[23]At present, we lack a principled explanation for the fact that only the bivalent version of the Applicative construction licenses state predications, since both the bivalent and trivalent Applicative constructions license atelic predications (viz., activities), and states belong to the class of atelic situations.

paraphrase in (5.91c) is, however acceptable, as the coverage constraint is not operative here:

(5.91) a. Ekkehard **bewohnt** ein Apartment in Berlin.
'Ekkehard *be*-lives an apartment in Berlin.'

b. *Ekkehard **bewohnt** Berlin.
'Ekkehard *be*-lives Berlin.'

c. Ekkehard **wohnt in** Berlin.
'Ekkehard lives in Berlin.'

Within the class of perfective applicatives, both accomplishment and processual (activity) readings are attested. These two readings are closely aligned semantically, since accomplishments entail processes. Nonpunctual perfective verbs (e.g., *walk*) typically have both activity and accomplishment readings, and the same can be said of bivalent applicative sentences like (5.88), which have both telic and atelic readings. If the interpreter views the sailing activity as having culminated in thorough coverage of the body of water by the sailor's craft, the predication denotes an accomplishment. If instead the interpreter construes the sailing activity as a set of subevents with no inherent point of culmination, the predication denotes an activity (as expressed by the processual gloss 'sail around'). Because these two readings are available, both types of durational adverbials are licensed, as shown in (5.92a). Since bivalent applicatives denote both processual and static situations, the coverage schema in our framework cannot be equated with the concept of an incrementally interpreted location argument. Trivalent applicative predications, which are necessarily perfective, generally have accomplishment readings, as in (5.92b). In such cases our analysis overlaps with Brinkmann's analysis (as described in section 2.3.2): the location argument is incremental in the sense of Dowty (1991), since its 'exhaustion' determines the time course of the event. However, trivalent applicative predications do not always require telic construals and do not always permit them. The telic construal appears to be required only when the base verb is telic (contingent upon a bounded construal of the object-denotatum), as in the case of *laden*. The trivalent applicative predication in (5.92c), which contains the atelic base verb *werfen* 'throw', does not have a telic interpretation:

(5.92) a. Sie **besegelten** die Karibik { in drei Monaten / drei Monate lang }.
'They *be*-sailed
{ the Caribbean in three months / around the Carribean for three months }.'

b. Sie **belud** den Wagen { in drei Stunden / *drei Stunden lang }.
'She *be*-loaded the wagon { in three hours / *for three hours }.'

c. Sicherheitskräfte wurden { *in drei Stunden / drei Stunden lang } mit Steinen **beworfen** .
'Security forces were pelted (lit. *be*-thrown) with stones { *in three hours / for three hours }.'

Numerous acts of transfer occur in the course of the event denoted by (c), and yet there is no point at which transfer is complete. Thus, while the trivalent applicative construction denotes a transfer event, insofar as an agent causes a theme to move to a location, this event type has both telic and atelic instantiations. Accordingly, the term *transfer event*, like the term *coverage*, should not be taken to entail that an endpoint is reached. The trivalent applicative construction is unmarked with respect to telicity, and only predicate-argument structure fixes aspectual class.

As pointed out earlier, entailments shared by two situation types may be manifested in common morphosyntactic coding. Transfer has cognate concept, removal, which is expressed by the trivalent applicative pattern as well. In the case of transfer and removal, the shared entailment is causation of change of location, and languages like Latin appear to neutralize the direction of transfer, coding the two event types identically. For example, trivalent verbs like *compleo* 'fill' and *privo* 'strip' license the same case frame, with the possibility of either ablative or genitive coding for the oblique theme argument Michaelis (1993). In German, removal verbs coded by the applicative pattern typically denote robbing, e.g., *bemopsen*, *berauben*, and *beklauen*. An example involving *beklauen* is given in (5.93):

(5.93) 36891726
Allein die Gelnhäuser Stadthalle habe das Trio zweimal **beklaut**, berichtete ein Kriposprecher am Donnerstag .
'A police spokesman reported on Thursday that the trio robbed (*be*-robbed) the Gelnhausen City Hall twice.'

Like the trivalent *be*-predications denoting coverage, *be*-predications denoting removal can be said to denote a salient effect upon the location argument. However, applicative verbs of removal differ from applicative verbs of coverage in that the former form a small class with idiosyncratic properties. For example, applicative verbs of removal do not typically license an obliquely expressed theme argument. Compare (5.94), which contains the nonapplicative verb *klauen* 'steal', with (5.95), an ill-formed variant of (5.93) in which the theme argument is expressed:

(5.94) Allein aus/von der Gelnhäuser Stadthalle habe das Trio zweimal Geld **geklaut**, berichtete ein Kriposprecher am Donnerstag.
'A police spokesman reported on Thursday that the trio stole money from the Gelnhausen City Hall twice.'

(5.95) *Allein die Gelnhäuser Stadthalle habe das Trio zweimal um 1000 Mark **beklaut**, berichtete ein Kriposprecher am Donnerstag .
'A police spokesman reported on Thursday that the trio robbed the Gelnhausen City Hall of 1000 marks twice.'

In (5.95), we use a preposition phrase headed by *um* 'around' to express the oblique theme (rather than, say, a PP headed by *von* 'of' or *mit* 'with') on analogy with the applicative verb *betrügen* 'cheat'. This verb, although arguably a verb of removal, does license an *um*-headed PP denoting the theme (the item which the victim loses to the cheater). Neither this fact about *betrügen* nor the more general theme-coding constraint exemplified in (5.95) follows from anything that we know about removal. That small verb clusters like the removal class should behave idiosyncratically is expected under Goldberg's (1995) model of partial productivity, to be discussed in section 5.5. Goldberg suggests that the association between a given construction and a given verb from a low-productivity class may be learned as an idiom (1995:132).

5.2 Metaphorical Extensions of the Central Sense

The coverage schema associated with the basic usage of the applicative pattern is compatible not only with concrete physical situations but also abstract ones. Langacker describes the basis of such semantic broadening as follows: "Extensions from the prototype occur [...] because of our proclivity for interpreting the new or less familiar with reference to what is already well established; and from the pressure of adapting a limited inventory of conventional units to the unending, ever-varying parade of situations requiring linguistic expression" (1991:295). Various metaphorical links allow the use of the saturation semantics in the domains of speech, perception, and attention. In accordance with Lakoff's (1990) Invariance Hypothesis, by which ontological components of a basic-level semantic schema are conserved by metaphorical extensions of that schema, we can observe that these metaphorical mappings replicate the thematic and linking structure associated with the bivalent applicative construction. We treat these metaphorical usages as distinct (conventionalized) senses of the *be*-pattern because otherwise there would be no way of predicting which theoretically eligible metaphors would be expressed by the *be*-pattern and which would not. In the following three subsections, we describe three metaphorical extensions.

5.2.1 Seeing is Contact with the Percept

One's gaze goes from one's eyes to what one sees. One sees whatever one's gazes touches (Lakoff 1987:437). These metaphors underlie German usages like the following:

(5.96) Sie konnte ihre Augen nicht von ihm nehmen
'She wasn't able to take her eyes off him.'

(5.97) Er richtete seinen Blick auf das Buch.
'He turned [directed] his eyes to the book.'

(5.98) GR1/TL1.12150 Weyden, C.: Träume sind wie der Wind.
'Ich hoffe es.' Und wieder ging sein Blick zu dem anderen Tisch hinüber.
'I hope so'. And another glance went over to the other table.'

Verbs, prepositions, and particles that are used to designate a trajcctor's movement to a physical object can be extended metaphorically to designate a metaphorical trajector's movement across the field of vision (cast a stone at—cast a glance at; point a weapon at—point one's eyes at). According to this model, INSPECTION of a percept is thorough coverage of the percept by the perceiver. In *be*-predications that denote vision, the eyes are construed as a theme moving over the percept. The following *be*-predications instantiate this particular conception:

(5.99) BZK/W59.00790, WE 07.09.59, S.06, Leserbriefe
Niemand sollte sich den Gang zum alten Museum ersparen. Man muß einmal Zeit genug haben, den Isenheimer Altar des Meisters Matthies zu **beschauen**, den ganzen Riesenaufbau in all seiner Wucht und Farbentiefe.
'Nobody should avoid the walk to the old museum. For once, one has to spend enough time to examine (lit. *be*-look) the Isenheimer altar of master Matthies, the whole gigantic body in all its massiveness and depth of color.'

(5.100) MK1/LFH.00000, Frisch, Homo Faber, Roman. Suhrkamp
Später auf Deck äußerte Sabeth (ohne Drängen meinerseits) den Wunsch, einmal den Maschinenraum zu **besichtigen**, und zwar mit mir [...]

'Later on deck Sabeth expressed the wish (without me urging her) to tour (lit. *be*-sight) the engine-room, and to do so with me [...]'

Although one might presume from the description of the metaphor that the agent maps to the perceiver and the theme to the gaze, the two roles are not obviously distinct, and we have found no *be*-predications in which the gaze/theme maps to an oblique expression. Insofar as the perceiver is difficult to separate from his or her perception, the agent and theme roles appear to conflate, and only the bivalent *be*-pattern is involved. The verbs in (5.99-5.100) have an elaboration relation to the applicative construction, since the perceiver and percept arguments map to theme and location, respectively. The joint fusion of the perceiver and the means of perception with the theme argument is a general characteristic of examples involving perception, including those which involve coverage of the percept via other sensory modalities:

(5.101) Message ID <6vdjTb12mnB@sampo.han.de>
Als Nichtraucher behaupte ich, daß sie nicht "stinken". Immerhin hatte ich auch schon Gelegenheit, Raucherinnen aus ziemlicher Nähe **beriechen** zu können. Ergebnis: sie stinken nicht.
'As a [male] non-smoker I say that they [smokers] do not "stink". At least, I have had the opportunity to *be*-sniff female smokers from rather close distance. Conclusion: they don't stink.'

5.2.2 Attending to Something is Directing One's Attention to it

Conventional examples of this metaphor are given in (5.102-5.104):

(5.102) Er richtete seine Gedanken auf das Thema.
'He directed his thoughts to the topic.'

(5.103) Seine Gedanken schweiften ab.
'His thoughts went astray.'

(5.104) Wohin gehen Ihre Überlegungen?
'What are you thinking of (lit. Where are your thoughts going to) ?'

Via this metaphor, tracking or monitoring a percept can be viewed as maintaining contact with it across a set of space-time coordinates, where the emergent configuration involves coverage of the region defined by that cluster of points. This conception underlies bivalent denominal *be*-predications like the following, in which, as in the vision case in 5.2.1, the cognizer and the cognizer's focus of attention are conflated and jointly fuse with the role of theme:

(5.105) Der Polizist **beobachtete** den Verdächtigen.
'The policeman watched (lit. *be*-observationed) the suspect.'

(5.106) Peter muß seine kleine Schwester **beaufsichtigen**, wenn seine Eltern zur Arbeit sind.
'Peter has to look after (lit. *be*-supervision) his little sister when his parents are at work.'

(5.107) Peter hat den Unfall verursacht, weil er die Vorfahrt nicht **beachtete**.
'Peter caused the accident because he didn't pay attention to (lit. *be*-attention) the right of way.'

5.2.3 Discourse is Travel Across a Topic

Other *be*-predications express metaphorical mappings via the TRAVEL METAPHOR: mental activity and conversation are both movement through some metaphorical space, the space being identified with the subject-matter of thought or speech (Sweetser 1987, 1990). We find this travel metaphor in German usages like (5.108):

(5.108) Auf dieses Thema müssen wir noch einmal zurückkommen.
'We will have to come back to this topic.'

In these metaphorical usages we find verbs, particles, and prepositions extended from their original domain of physical movement to the domain of movement in speech or thought. Such metaphorical situations may be expressed by *be*-predications when the saturation implication is prominent, i.e. when the theme (the conversant) covers the location (the topic) comprehensively. Compare sentence (5.109), which describes a serious discussion, to sentence (5.110), which describes the conversational efforts of two previously unacquainted people on a first date:

(5.109) R1/TL1.09008 de Groot, B.: Dein Vater wird uns liebgewinnen.
Nebenan befand sich Olga Gorenkamps Nähzimmer, die Tür war nur angelehnt. Jetzt **besprachen** sie eingehend die neue Situation. Und sie war äußerst günstig für das Weingut.
'Next door was Olga Glorenkamp's sewing room. The door was ajar. Now they were discussing (lit. *be*-speaking) the new situation thoroughly. And it was extremely favorable for the winery.'

(5.110) MK1/LJA.00000, Johnson, Das dritte Buch über Achim
Karsch sagte ja. Er war erstaunt, daß sie gebeten hatte. Sie verabredeten sich für einen Abend, an dem ein Fubballspiel viele Fahrzeuge aus der Umgebung heranholen und dann wieder auf die Autobahn schicken würde, sie trafen sich vor dem Theater, **sprachen über** die Unterschiede der beiden deutschen Strabenbilder, fuhren los .
'Karsch said yes. He was surprised that she had asked. They made an appointment for an evening when a soccer game would attract a lot of cars from the surrounding area and send them back on the highway later. They met in front of the theater, spoke about how different the street looked in the two Germanies, and then drove off.'

The relationship between thorough discussion and coverage of a surface is evident a well in the English contrast between talking something *over* and talking *about* something.

5.3 Non-metaphorical Extensions

In addition to the metaphorical uses of the central senses which we discussed in 5.2. there are extensions of the central senses in which the coverage semantics is either missing or of secondary importance. Most of these extensions seem to be the result of pragmatic inferences like those described by Hopper and Traugott's (1993) model of PRAGMATIC STRENGTHENING, a metonymic inference mode by which a semantico-pragmatic 'side effect' of some signification is elevated to the level of a distinct meaning, which may lack entailments of the source meaning (see also König and Traugott 1988). An example of pragmatic strengthening is the development of concessive or adversative markers from markers of temporal persistence like *still*; the newly developed marker is usable in perfective predications, where no temporal continuation is implied, as in *She still got angry* König and Traugott (1988).

In the following four subsections, we will describe four meanings of the *be*-pattern which appear to involve this metonymic mode of inference: transfer, iteration, intensification, and affectedness. A fifth subsection will consider a class of denominal *be*-verbs expressing social roles, which appear to involve the affectedness meaning. The first class of cases, that of applicatives denoting transfer (5.3.1), deserves comment here because it is subject to dual categorizations: it is both a metaphorically based extension and an inference-based one. Since this class involves a metaphorical extension, thematic structure is isomorphic to that of the applicative construction, as in the metaphorically based extensions discussed in section 5.2. Predications which denote metaphorical transfer preserve the thematic and linking constraints associated with the (trivalent) applicative construction: they entail an agent, a nonoblique goal and a (canonically null-instantiated) theme. However, this metaphorical extension is based upon a prototypical rather than necessary component of the coverage schema: transfer. For this reason, the coverage entailment which plays a role in other metaphorical uses of the applicative pattern plays no role here. The remaining pragmatically based extensions to be discussed in this section are nonmetaphorical. They are based solely on marginal implications of the applicative pattern, and do not partake directly of the semantics of location or transfer. These extensions thereby lack the thematic and linking constraints associated with the applicative pattern. These extensions meet only the valency and morphological conditions on applicatives: they are bivalent and thereby compatible with the transitive linking construction described in chapter 4.

5.3.1 Communication and Affecting as Transfer

Applicative predications may describe situations in which metaphorical objects are transferred to a goal or recipient. This sense can be viewed as an extension of the meaning of the trivalent *be*-pattern, in which saturation comes about through transfer of a concrete theme onto a location, e.g., *behängen* '*be*-hang', *beladen* '*be*-load', *bedecken* '*be*-cover'. In its metaphorical transfer sense, however, the *be*-construction does not entail saturation; transfer is the sole entailment. One kind of metaphorical theme is an idea. Via the IDEAS ARE TRANSFERABLE OBJECTS metaphor and the complex CONDUIT metaphor of communication Reddy (1979), the *be*-construction can be used to describe communication events. The agent is a person delivering the idea, the idea is the theme, and the recipient is the goal. The *be*-construction evokes this metaphor in the following example:

(5.111) Message ID <22D3C5E8H000002AFH@p-alv.wds.mcnet.de>
Er hatte niemals daran gedacht, sie zu fragen oder sie auch nur zu **benachrichtigen**, daß er Clarisse für verschwunden hielt.
'He had never remembered to ask her or to even inform her (lit. *be*-news) her that he considered Clarisse to have disappeared.'

The metaphor can be made explicit in the sentence's paraphrase:

(5.112) [...] oder ihnen auch nur Nachricht darüber zu geben, daß er [...]
lit. '[...] or to just give them news about the fact that he [...]'

It also occurs independently of situations which can be described by *be*-predications in such usages as:

(5.113) Er sandte mir einen Gruß.
'He sent me greetings.'

Another metaphorical link to the domain of transfer is provided by the EFFECTS ARE TRANSFERRED OBJECTS metaphor (Goldberg 1995: ch. 6). The use of the *be*-construction to express this metaphor may be seen as doubly motivated: first by the fact that literal uses of the (trivalent) applicative pattern involve transfer and second by the fact that coverage of a location often involves an effect upon that location. Consider the following denominal example:

(5.114) WKB/TZ1.00567, *taz* (Sonderheft 1 und 2)
[...] versuchte die Partei mit ihrem anfänglichen unverbindlichen Dialogangebot vergeblich den demonstrativen Unmut der Bevölkerung einzudämmen, so hofft sie jetzt, die Konflikte am runden Tisch zu kanalisieren und das Volk zu **befrieden**.
'[...] if the party tried in vain to contain the ostentatious ill humor of the population with their initially non-binding offer of a dialog, it is now hoping to channel the conflicts at the round table and to bring peace to (lit. *be*-peace) the people.'

In this example, the source nominal (*Frieden*) denotes a transferable effect. Transferable effects include properties, as expressed by deadjectival applicative predications like (5.115)(=(2.15)):

(5.115) *Süddeutsche Zeitung*, March 4, 1996
Deutsche Grenzschützer **befreiten** die Geiseln am 18. Oktober 1977 in Mogadischu; Andrawes überlebte als einziger der Terroristen.
'Members of the German border patrol freed (lit. *be*-freed) the hostages on October 18, 1977 in Mogadishu; Andrawes was the only one of the terrorists to survive.'

These denominal and deadjectival applicative verbs lack base forms. Therefore, it is plausible to assume that their meanings come from the integration of constructional and lexical frame semantics via the elaboration relation, in much the same way that a transfer implication attaches to denominal applicatives which express coverage of a surface, e.g., *behaaren* '*be*-hair' and *beschildern* '*be*-signpost'. In both the literal (coverage) cases and the metaphorical cases in (5.114-5.115), the lexical item which unifies with the construction is construed as a transfer verb via implicit conversion, and the oblique theme is null instantiated owing to its recoverability. The examples in (5.116-5.117) show that the transfer of abstract effects is a special case of a general model in which effects of all kinds, including physical ones, are transferable from an agent onto a patient-goal:

(5.116) Message ID <782aug*gr*51@infosun2.rus.uni-stuttgart.de>
Jeder will dem Gegner so schnell wie möglich eine tiefe blutende Wunde beibringen, ihn 'abstechen', wie es im Jargon der schlagenden Verbindungen heißt
'Each wants to inflict on the opponent a deep bleeding wound (lit. bring the opponent a deep bleeding wound) as fast he can, that is 'stick' him, as they say in the jargon of dueling fraternities.'

(5.117) Message ID <4tsk0s$n4m@ra.ibr.cs.tu-bs.de> Schaden können diese Bücher einem nicht zufügen.
'These books can't do any harm to people (lit. add harm to people).'

5.3.2 Iteration

Iteration is a frequent concomitant of concrete uses of the central sense. We saw that predications involving saturation typically involve multiple instances of a given action. For example, predications involving *beladen* '*be*-load' often express scenarios in which many items are loaded in succession. However, the notion of iteration can also be expressed by *be*-verbs independently of the transfer or saturation implications. Example (5.118) illustrates this:

(5.118) 8805296:
Es kann nicht angehen, daß auch auf kommunaler Ebene Wahlbeamte schon mit vierzig eine Pension **beziehen**.
'It cannot be the case that even on the municipal level elected officals draw (lit. *be*-draw) a pension already at the age of 40.'

This examples illustrates the use of the verb *ziehen* 'pull, draw' in the applicative pattern to denote regular reception of goods or funds (as when one subscribes to a newspaper or receives retirement income). Example (5.119) presents another case in which an applicative predication prominently expresses iteration:

(5.119) MMM/912.44101: *Mannheimer Morgen*, 03.12.1989, Sonstiges
Puppen aus Porzellan mit echtem Lockenkopf und zarten Sommersprösschen gehören für 700 Mark in jede Schicky-Micky-Kinderstube, zumindest eine Käthe-Kruse, trotz des bäuerlichen Gesichtsausdruck ein Prestige-Objekt für höhere Töchter muß her, obgleich vielleicht eine kitschige Barbie im überladenen Nylon-Abendkleid viel mehr geliebt und **bespielt** wird.

'For 700 marks porcelain dolls with real curly hair and delicate freckles should be part of every fancy-shmancy playroom; for daughters of the upper-class it has to be at least a Kaethe Kruse—an object of prestige in spite of the rustic physiognomy—although a kitschy Barbie doll in a pretentious nylon evening dress might be loved and played with (lit. *be*-played) much more.'

In example (5.119) the *be*-playing predication does not entail that a given doll might become worn out and ragged as a result of playing. It is also difficult to detect a coverage implication here, since a doll is not a surface which one can cover by means of playing, as in the *bespielen* predication in (5.127) below. Instead, what is relevant is the frequency with which the child is likely to play with the Barbie doll. Examples like (5.119) illustrate the circumstances under which the iteration implication—otherwise a happenstance concomitant of the coverage implication conventionally associated with the applicative pattern—comes to be the sole implication expressed by the *be*-pattern. The iteration implication is the sole feature responsible for contrast pairs like *hindern* 'stop, prevent' vs. *behindern* 'hinder'. By assuming an iteration use of the *be*-pattern, we account for a usage of the verb *befahren* which otherwise appears to violate a robust constraint on the applicative pattern: the location must be two-dimensional (see section 3.5). Use of *befahren* to describe car travel appears to violate the planar-location constraint, because the locative argument (the roadway) is a one-dimensional rather than two-dimensional location. Examples (5.120-5.121) illustrate this usage:

(5.120) Message ID <7ABkUTL9WpB@kholdan.snafu.de>
Kennst du die Unfallstatistiken jeder solcher Straßen? Weißt du ganz sicher, wieviele Unfälle dort schon passiert sind?

Wenn ich täglich paarmal eine Straße **befahre**? Klar.

'Do you know the accident statistics of all such streets? Do you know for sure how many accidents have happened there already?

If I *be*-drive that road a few times per day? Of course.'

(5.121) Message ID <3716ad43.95796920@news.nacamar.de>
Heute stand mal wieder an einer Straße, die ich oft **befahre**, ein schöner Zivil-Passat mit zwei Leuten drin und einem seltsamen viereckigen Gerät in der Hand ;-)

'Today a nice unmarked Passat happened to park along a road that I *be*-drive often. In it were two people with a strange rectangular device in their hands.'

The uses in (5.120-5.121) are unexpected because they invoke a distinct construal from that associated with the applicative predication involving the sailor and the Baltic Sea in (4.85) above: in the two above examples there is no two-dimensional location for the driver (and vehicle) to thoroughly cover. The applicative predications in these examples certainly do not lead one to construct a scenario in which a driver is 'covering' the road by swerving her car to the left and right. Nor is there any notion that the driver is driving with particular intensity. Similarly, it is not implied that the road is affected more heavily by *be*-driving than by some other kind of driving. Rather what is crucial for the uses of *befahren* in examples (5.120) and (5.121) is that driving represents an iterated activity.[24] One may, for instance, *be*-drive a particular road to work every day. That iteration is crucial to the use of *befahren* to describe car travel is suggested by speakers' preference for (5.122a) over (5.122b):

(5.122) a. *Ich **befahre** heute die A3.
'I'll take/drive on highway A3 today.'
b. Ich **fahre** heute die A3.
'I'll take/drive on highway A3 today.'

The relationship between verb semantics and construction semantics in examples like (5.120-5.121) appears to be that of elaboration, since the verb and the construction are each bivalent. In the case of (5.119), the player and the 'instrument' roles assigned by the verb *spielen* 'play' map to the agent and theme roles assigned by (this sense of) the construction. The elaboration relation is identified when the verb is a more specific instance of the event type designated by the construction. Does this characterization apply to the iteration usage? The applicative construction designates a sequence of iterated events, whereas the verb *spielen*,

[24]There is, however, an idiomatic use of *befahren* which lacks the iteration implication. It is associated with reports on traffic accidents and easily identifiable by the fact that in the overwhelming majority of cases the direction in which the driver was driving on the road is given. An example of this idiomatic usage is the following:

4321018
Einem Bad Nauheimer Autofahrer, der am Freitag gegen 14.40 Uhr die Wetteraustraße in Dorheim in Richtung Wölfersheim befuhr, lief ein achtjähriges Mädchen direkt vor den Wagen.
'An 8-year old girl ran right in front of the car of a driver from Bad Nauheim who was driving down (lit. *be*-driving) Wetteraustreet in Dorheim towards Wölfersheim.'

e.g., does not denote a sequence of iterated playing events. However, insofar as the verb denotes the event type which is replicated in the constructional semantics, we can identify an elaboration relation in this case.

5.3.3 Intensification

Numerous *be*-predications share the notion of intensive action but do not involve coverage of any surface. This intensification sense may be attributed to a pragmatic inference of the following kind. Many *be*-predications entail repetition of subevents. The repetition of subevents is evidence that the activity is carried out with greater intensity than in the case of comparable isolated events. While we lack diachronic evidence for a path of grammaticalization along these lines, it is plausible in the light of other findings. For instance, Regier (1994), in a typological study of the semantics of reduplication, links the INTENSITY-sense of reduplication to the PLURALITY-sense, which in turn is linked to the claimed central sense, REPETITION. An example of a *be*-predication which exhibits the intensification sense is *besiegen* 'defeat'. As shown in the following example, *besiegen* expresses a more decisive resolution of a conflict than does *siegen über* 'be victorious over':

(5.123) MK1/WJA.00000, Jaspers, Die Atombombe und die Zukunft des Menschen
Sollte Rußland den Krieg beginnen—etwa durch Überschreitung der Grenze nach dem Westen, so würde seinen Massenheeren, die mit den konventionellen Waffen Europa schnell **besiegen** könnten, wahrscheinlich sofort mit Atomwaffen begegnet.
'Should Russia start the war—say by crossing the border to the West—its mass armies, which would be able to defeat Europe quickly with conventional weapons, would likely be immediately responded to with nuclear weapons.'

Similarly, *bekämpfen* differs from *kämpfen* 'fight' in implying higher intensity: one is not simply fighting against something, but actively combating something.

(5.124) 1028294
Die Naturschutzgruppe hält daher Vorschläge bereit, wie man Schädlinge natürlich, ohne Einsatz von chemischen Giften, **bekämpfen** kann.
'The environmentalist group therefore offers suggestions on how you can combat (lit. *be*-fight) pests naturally, without the use of chemical poisons.'

While the type of action that *bekämpfen* 'combat' expresses involves repeated engagements, the iteration notion is not by itself enough to warrant the use of this verb: an event involving a series of defensive battles could not be described by this verb. Thus, it is the intensification notion that appears to be relevant to the usage of this verb. Further examples of the intensification function are given in (5.125-5.126). The base forms of the applicative verb shown here are *schimpfen* 'scold' and *fürchten* 'be afraid of'. *Beschimpfen* denotes abusive verbal behavior. *Befürchten* denotes an enhanced state of dread, involving a possible past or future state or event.[25]. Example (5.126) shows that the intensification function of the applicative need not have any implication of iterated action, since here it is a state predicate which is intensified.

(5.125) 18141081
Es berechtigt sie weder, die Polizei zu **beschimpfen** und mit Steinen zu bewerfen, noch eine bunte Palette von Wurfgeschossen in Richtung Innenraum zu schleudern.
'It doesn't give them the right to verbally abuse (lit. *be*-scold) the police and pelt them with stones nor to hurl all manner of projectiles in the direction of the interior.'

(5.126) 339815
Dies lasse für den bevorstehenden Kommunalwahlkampf Schlimmes **befürchten**.
'This would be reason to fear (lit. *be*-fear) bad things during the upcoming local election campaign'.

The relation between the verb and (this usage of) the applicative construction is again that of elaboration: the verb is a subtype of the situation type denoted by the construction. The situation type denoted by the construction corresponds to an extreme point on a scale for eventualities, whether these are actions (like gaining victories or scolding) or states (like fearing).

5.3.4 Affectedness

One can define affectedness as a change of physical or mental state which is (potentially or actually) effected by some action. A location is potentially affected by the theme's movement across it, as in (5.127):

[25] As an anonymous reviewer pointed out, simple *fürchten*, unlike *befürchten* can be a disposition, for instance towards dogs (*Er (*be)fürchtet Hunde* 'He's afraid of dogs').

(5.127) MMM/507.07898: *Mannheimer Morgen*, 14.07.1995, Lokales
Die Frage, ob der Mundenheimer Platz **bespielbar** ist, wird künftig der Platzwart entscheiden. Eine kleine Einschränkung bleibt: Die Stadt behält sich das Recht vor, anders zu entscheiden, wenn Gefahr besteht, daß das Spielfeld erheblich beeinträchtigt werden könnte
'The question whether the Mundenheimer Field can be played on (lit. is *be*-playable) will in future be decided by the groundsman. But a small restriction remains: the city reserves the right to decide otherwise if there is a danger that the field could be damaged considerably.'

AFFECTEDNESS is a frequent concomitant of SATURATION: damage to the soccer field results from the players' sequential or summary coverage of the field. As we pointed out earlier, however, saturation does not entail affectedness. For instance, in the static *bewohnen* '*be*-live' scenario denoted by sentence (5.90), repeated here as (5.128), the inhabitants of the town center of Altriper do not necessarily affect their surroundings through their habitation:

(5.128) MMM/102.37001: *Mannheimer Morgen*, 09.02.1991, Leserbriefe
Die alteingesessenen Altriper, die den Ortskern bis jetzt noch **bewohnen**, werden sich eben mit dem noch stärker werdenden Durchgangsverkehr abfinden müssen.
'The long-time Altriperians who up until now are still living in (lit. *be*-living) the town center will just have to get used to the increasing through traffic.'

There is here no implication that the inhabitants wear out their homes or the streets in their neighborhood. (The notion of abuse through habitation is in fact lexicalized separately by the verb *abwohnen*, lit. 'live down'.) Thus coverage does not entail a change of state in the location, although affectedness is a frequent implication of predications involving coverage. We contend that this implication is the basis for an extended usage of the applicative pattern in which only affecting and not coverage is entailed. Predications which exemplify this usage express the means by which the effect is achieved. For example, most speech-act verbs can be used in the applicative pattern to denote a means of annoying the recipient:

(5.129) *Süddeutsche Zeitung* , November 28, 1992
HEADLINE: Die Leute wollen sich nicht **belabern** lassen. n-tv-Geschäftsführer. Karl-Ulrich Kuhlo über die Chancen seines Nachrichtenprogramms, das am Montag auf Sendung geht.

'HEADLINE: People don't want to be blathered at (lit. *be*-blathered). N-tv executive Karl-Ulrich Kuhlo about the prospects for his news channel, which goes on the air Monday.'

These uses of speech-act verbs do not appear to be based upon a metaphorical mapping whose source domain involves saturation or coverage, e.g., the SPEECH IS TRAVEL ACROSS A TOPIC metaphor. Instead, speech-act verbs in examples like (5.129) express the means by which an effect is achieved. While in (5.129) this effect is unintended, the effect may also be an intended one, as in (5.130):

(5.130) Message ID <3779D77E.EC802A73@fh-konstanz.de>
Meistens muß man den selber einbauen. Außer du bist sehr gut im Leute **bequatschen**.
'In most cases you have to install it yourself. Except if you're very good at persuading (lit. *be*-talking) people.'

Applicative verbs of domestic and culinary activity also frequently express the means by which a (beneficial) effect is achieved. Sentence (5.131) (a response to an on-line personals ad) exemplifies this usage of the applicative for the verbs *kochen* 'cook' and *putzen* 'clean':

(5.131) Message ID <35666380.12664736@news.netway.at>
Und wenn Du [...] arbeitest, mir das Geld ins Haus trägst, mach' ich die Kinder (gebären müßtest Du sie bitte), mach' ich den Haushalt, **bekoch'** dich (und hoffe Dir schmeckt's), **beputz'** Dich (waschen mußt' Dich selber), und halt' Dir die Kinder vom Leib.
'And if you work [...] and bring home the money, then I'll take care of the kids (you just have to give birth), I'll take care of the house, I'll *be*-cook you (hope you like what I cook), *be*-clean you (you have to wash yourself yourself), and keep the kids out of your way.'

Crucially, the role of the object-denotatum is that of beneficiary rather than theme. The theme argument licensed by the verb can be expressed by an oblique, as in the example of *bekochen* in (1.1), ([...] *habe ich mich* [...] *mit Kaffee bekochen lassen* '[...] I had myself *be*-cooked with coffee'. However, this oblique could be analyzed as an instrumental adjunct, as it clearly is in (5.132):

(5.132) Message ID <36969A47.ADA335C0@gmx.net>
Ich habe sogar vor, meine Wohnebene (Uni) am Wochenende als Versuchskaninchen zu benutzen. Ich habe schon Tage lang nach einem guten Rezept gesucht, mit dem ich meine Mitstudenten am Wochenende **bekochen** kann.

> 'I am even planning on using the people on my floor (college dormitory) as guinea pigs. I have been looking for days now for a good recipe with which I can *be*-cook my fellow students over the weekend.'

The theme is not construable as an instrument in the case of *beputzen*, and an oblique theme is accordingly ruled out: **Die Haushälterin beputze mich mit der Küche* 'The housekeeper *be*-cleaned me with the kitchen'. It is not obvious, however, why an oblique theme should require an instrumental construal, since it does not necessarily receive one. Because the oblique theme is licensed by the Oblique Theme construction, the grammaticality contrast at issue here appears to hinge on the applicability of that construction. As represented in chapter 4, the Oblique Theme construction denotes a transfer event. However, we have said that the version of the Applicative construction which carries the affectedness implication is bivalent, and owes nothing directly to the semantics of transfer. Since, however, we allow linking constructions to augment verbal valence, with concomitant semantic effects, there seems to be no reason to prevent the Oblique Goal construction from combining with the bivalent applicative pattern which denotes affecting, adding a theme argument and imposing a construal in which the benefactive activity entails transfer. Insofar as culinary activity entails transfer to the beneficiary, this construal is coherent. Since benefaction via cleaning does not entail transfer, unification of *beputzen* with the Oblique-Theme construction does not yield a coherent construal.[26]

The affectedness implication associated with applicative sentences like (5.131-5.132) is typically associated either with an iteration implication, as when habitual beneficial activity is denoted (5.131), or a coverage implication, as when a bounded set of individuals is serviced (5.132). The affectedness, coverage and iteration implications may be present simultaneously, as in (5.133):

[26]Both *putzen* and *kochen* take incremental themes; only *bekochen*, however, allows the theme to receive a deindividuated construal when expressed as an oblique. This suggests a necessary condition on oblique linking for themes: the theme must be construable as deindividuated, as per Brinkmann's Nonindividuation Hypothesis. Such a constraint would explain the ill formedness of resultative examples like **She cleaned herself into a frenzy with the house* and the German example **Die Haushälterin beputzte mich mit der Küche* 'The housekeeper *be*-cleaned me with the kitchen'. However, any theme is in principle construable as deindividuated—via pluralization in the case of singular count nouns, for example. The combination of *beputzen* with an oblique theme is equally ill formed when that theme is unbounded: **Sie beputzen Leute mit Küchen* 'They *be*-clean people with [their] kitchens'. Therefore, we presume that the restriction on oblique themes among applicative verbs of domestic activity hinges on the validity of the transfer implication rather than a constraint involving deindividuation.

(5.133) www.tagesspiegel.de/ressorts/portrait/B/BONA400.HTM
Täglich holen einige Obdachlose aus der Teestube frische Brötchen und Kuchen in der Bäckerei ab. 60-80 Menschen zu **bebacken**, kostet Bonau und seine Mitarbeiter am Tag eine gute Viertelstunde Arbeit. Das ist—laut Bonau—nicht der Rede wert.
'Every day some homeless people from the tea room pick up fresh rolls and cake in the bakery. To *be*-bake 60-80 people takes Bonau and his employees fifteen minutes of work per day. That's hardly worth mentioning, says Bonau.'

In (5.133), a coverage interpretation is possible because the group of beneficiaries, via its cardinality, 'measures out' the baking event—this event is completed when all of the individuals in the group are provided for. Since the event (as described) is iterated daily, the iteration implication is present here as well. The mutual compatibility of the (otherwise separable) coverage, affectedness and iteration implications in the interpretation of (5.133) is unsurprising on the present account, since each of these notions belongs to a single coherent event schema. However, nonce formations like (5.134) show that there are productive uses of the applicative pattern which exploit the affectedness implication alone:

(5.134) *Süddeutsche Zeitung*, May 27, 1995
[...] und während einem die heißen Rhythmen der kubanischen Musik in die Glieder fahren, strömen lächelnde Mädchen, zweifelsfrei Sendboten eines fernen Planeten der Freude, in die graue Welt, von vorne, von hinten, von den Seiten, angetan mit Flitter und Tand, mit Federbüschen und Riesenblumen, mit Durchsichtigem und Undurchsichtigem, und sie **betanzen** dich, behexen dich, verwirren dich, machen dir warm ums Herz, und das 30-Mann-Orchester spielt wie entfesselt, und in den bunten Nebeln baden in natürlicher Eleganz die Königinnen der Illusion.[27]
'[...] and while the hot rhythms of Cuban music get to you, smiling girls-undoubtedly messengers of a far away planet of joy-stream into the gray world from all sides, clad in tinsel and finery, plumes and giant flowers, in transparent and nontransparent clothes, and they *be*-dance you, bewitch you, confuse you, make you feel hot, and the 30-member orchestra plays as if in a rage, and the queens of illusion bask with natural elegance in the multi-colored mists.'

[27]Notice that *behexen* exemplifies the kind of extension discussed in the next section.

In the use of *betanzen* '*be*-dance' in (5.134) the beneficiary receives the accusative coding otherwise associated with the location argument, and therefore there is no notion of coverage of the stage, etc. The only semantic factor that links this use of *be-* to other senses is the implication of affectedness: the dancers affect the audience by means of their performance.

5.3.5 Act in a Particular Capacity Toward Someone

This small group of denominal *be*-verbs includes *bemuttern* (< *Mutter* 'mother'), *bewirten* (< *Wirt* 'host'), *bespitzeln* (< *Spitzel* 'spy'), and *behexen* (< *Hexe* 'witch'). Examples are given in (5.135) and (5.136):

(5.135) Message ID <slrn6sf8ab.61.bones@castle.aball.de>
Männer möchten auch zuweilen dominiert (**bemuttert**) werden, dann brauchen sie nämlich auch nur zu empfangen und sind jeglicher Verantwortung (und Konsequenzen) enthoben.
'At times, men want to be dominated (*be*-mothered), too. For then they only have to receive and they are relieved of any responsibility (and consequences).'

(5.136) www.phil.uni-passau.de/dlwg/ws07/12-1-97.txt
Mesmer hatte die Heilung der (durch eine Lähmung des Sehnervs) erblindeten Klavierspielerin Paradis erzielt; der Fall machte um so mehr Aufsehen, als die junge, offenbar übernervöse Musikerin von der Kaiserin Maria Theresia **begönnert** wurde.
'Mesmer had succeeded in healing the pianist Paradis who had gone blind (due to paralysis of her optic nerve); the case drew all the more attention since the young, apparently hypernervous musician was patronized (lit. *be*-patroned) by the empress Maria Theresia.'

These verbs differ from other denominal *be*-verbs in an important respect: the source nominal does not express the type of the theme argument, as it does in the case of applicative verbs with literal transfer semantics, e.g., *beschildern* '*be*-sign' in (2.13) or in the case of applicative verbs which evoke the effects-as-transferred-objects metaphor, e.g., *befrieden* '*be*-peace' in (5.114). Instead, the nominal base in examples (5.135-5.136) expresses the type of role assumed by the AGENT of the event. The agent's assumption of this role is a precondition for achieving an effect upon the beneficiary. Therefore, we view this usage as inductively related to the affectedness usage discussed in 5.3.4: an agent may affect a beneficiary by assuming a particular role relative to that individual. This fairly weak inductive relationship is expressed by a semantic-extension link labeled *means* in Figure 9. This use of the term *means* is distinct from that in which the term refers to a particular verb-construction integration relation. The verb-construction integration relation which we assume for *bemuttern* and other applicatives of this class is the instance (or, equivalently, elaboration) relation. As in the case of denominals like *beschildern*, we postulate a type-shifting effect in which the base nominal receives a valence set via unification with the bivalent Applicative construction. The arguments in the valence set of the applicative construction fuse with the corresponding participant roles in the frame semantics of the particular noun. In the case of *bemuttern*, for example, these participant roles are the mother and the child. These frame-specific roles fuse with the corresponding roles licensed by the (bivalent) applicative construction. In accordance with our general treatment of denominal applicatives, we reject the view that the base noun, e.g., *Mutter*, 'denotes' a particular participant in the event expressed by the predication, in this case an agent. Instead, the source nominal denotes a type, permitting omission of the agent argument where type information is sufficient, as in (5.135).

5.4 Historical Evidence

The most plausible source for the semantics of coverage associated with the *be*-pattern is the 'around' schema associated with the historic precursor of *be*, the preposition *bi*. The modern English and German prepositions meaning 'around'—around and *um/herum* respectively—are ambiguous between a sense of 'surrounding an enclosed space' and 'being distributed over a surface area'. Consider the following data:

(5.137) Die Spieler versammelten sich um den Trainer.
'The players gathered around the coach.'

(5.138) Die Spieler standen auf dem Platz herum und warteten auf den Schlußpfiff.
'The players were standing around the pitch waiting for the final whistle.' (lit. '[...] around on the pitch [...]')

(5.139) Die Abwehrspieler liefen orientierungslos auf dem Platz herum.
'The defense were running around the pitch disoriented.' (lit. '[...] around on the pitch [...]')

In (5.137) we see that *um/herum* can denote a static surrounding configuration. Example (5.138) shows that *um/herum* can denote a static configuration involving coverage of a surface by multiple points. Example (5.139) demonstrates that the coverage scene expressed by *um/herum*, like that expressed by English *around*, is consistent with a dynamic scene in which a surface is covered over the course of time. The prefix *be-* had the set of senses that *um/herum* and *around* display in (5.137-5.139) through Grimm's time. Grimm lists Latin *circum* as the first sense for the *be*-prefix. But, as Ruppenhofer (1999) showed, *be*-verbs exemplifying the surrounding usage seen in (5.137) were already being lost in Grimm's time and continued to be lost thereafter. Among these lost verbs were, for instance, *bearmen* 'embrace'; *bezäunen* 'fence in'; and *behüllen* 'surround'. Only, a small number of *be*-verbs which denote surrounding or containment remain. Among these verbs is *beherbergen* 'shelter, harbor', which has both bivalent and trivalent uses. Bivalent *beherbergen* is exemplified in (5.140):

(5.140) 4037381
Das Schloßmuseum wurde 1908 eingerichtet und **beherbergt** außer prächtigen Stilmöbeln, englischen Gartenhockern und Leuchtern besonders kostbare Tafel- , Tee- und Kaffeeservices, geschmackvolles Geschirr und Porzellan-Zierat .
'The castle museum was established in 1908 and harbors (lit. *be*-shelters) particularly precious dinner, tea, and coffee services, tasteful dishes and porcelain ornaments in addition to magnificent period furniture, English garden seats, and chandeliers.'

Example (5.141) illustrates trivalent *beherbergen*:

(5.141) 9921167
Nach den Worten von Riebel **beherbergt** der Kreis bereits 1500 Asylbewerber in 55 Unterkünften.
'According to Riebel, the county is already providing accommodation to (lit. *be*-sheltering) 1500 asylum seekers in 55 shelters.'

Another clear example of the surrounding sense is *begrenzen* 'mark off, form the boundary of':

(5.142) 1093227
Als zukünftigen Standort schlägt die Friedberger CDU ein dem Wetteraukreis gehörendes Gelände vor, das westlich der Stadthalle liegt und **begrenzt** wird von der Ockstädter und Johann-Peter-Schäfer-Straße, dem Seebach und dem Parkplatz der Stadthalle.

'The Friedberg CDU [political party] proposes as future location an area belonging to Wetterau county that is delimited (lit. *be*-bordered) by Ockstädter Street and Johann-Peter-Schäfer Street, the Seebach [a brook], and the parking lot of the municipal hall.'

The surrounding sense of the prefix is no longer productive.[28] While the surrounding class might be regarded as a low-productivity verb cluster associated with the applicative pattern (along the lines of our treatment of the removal class in section 5.5), we chose to omit the surrounding class from our semantic analysis of the applicative pattern because the *be*-verbs which continue the semantics of enclosure do not share the linking constraints which we have identified with the applicative pattern. For example, the subject of bivalent (active) *beherbergen* is a location rather than a theme (as in (5.140)), and the object of trivalent (active) *beherbergen* is a theme rather than a location. While the surrounding sense of the *be*-prefix survives in a small set of verbs, the related sense of the prefix involving coverage of a surface is the basis of the productivity of the Applicative construction.[29]

By delineating the various entailments of the enclosure sense, we can understand not only the development of the coverage sense of *be*- but also the development of a PROXIMITY meaning which continues in the non-bound preposition *bei* and, like the surrounding sense, is preserved in a few *be*-verbs. Following Grimm (1854:1203), we treat the proximity meaning as having arisen by metonymy from the 'surrounding'-sense: what is in the vicinity of an object is close to it. An explanation along these lines is plausible since, for instance, the English preposition *around* has uses with the same implication of proximity, e.g. *John likes to be around his family.* The same is true for the Modern German preposition *um*, which also can be used in sentences like *Er hat seine Familie gerne um sich* 'He likes to have his family around him', where closeness to the theme or location rather than surrounding or enclosure of the theme is involved.

---

[28]Admittedly, however, the surrounding usage does appear to be the source of a limited number of denominal coinages. The verb *behausen* acquired its bivalent sense of 'house, shelter' only after Grimm's time. Also, *beheimaten* 'provide a home for' in both bivalent and trivalent form is unattested in Grimm. Since no other formations with a surrounding sense have occurred, we consider these developments as analogical extensions on the model of *beherbergen*.

[29]The 'around' meaning seems to have already been lost in Middle High German in the case of the related preposition *bî*, the source for Modern German *bei* 'by' (Lexer 1872).

Be-verbs which might be viewed as preserving the proximity semantics of the prefix are *bekommen* ‘get, obtain’, *belangen* ‘sue, prosecute’, *besteigen* ‘mount, climb, climb into’, and *betreten* ‘enter’, all of which are attested with such meanings in Middle High German (Lexer 1872). Literal glosses, which express the semantic contribution of the prefix, are, respectively: ‘come upon’ (as in the English verb *come by*, meaning ‘to obtain’), ‘reach toward’, ‘ascend to’, and ‘step onto’. Another class of verbs which appears to preserve the proximity-denoting sense of the prefix are statives which denote scenes in which a theme remains in place. Included within this class are: *behalten*, ‘keep’ (lit. ‘hold near’); *belassen*, ‘leave in place’, (lit. ‘leave by a place’); *beruhen*, ‘be based on’, (lit. ‘rest on’); and *bestehen*, ‘exist, insist’ (lit. ‘stand by a place’).

By treating the proximity, enclosure and coverage readings as components of a single semantic schema, we can account for a layering effect observable within the class of *be*-verbs: while the majority of *be*-verbs (and the totality of coinages in our corpus data) express notions related to the coverage component, certain small classes continue meanings associated with other components of that schema. As shown by the examples involving English and German *um/herum*, the patterns of semantic extension proposed both here and by Grimm for the *be*-prefix are plausible. These patterns collectively define a continuum of idiomaticity in the modern language: some instances of the applicative pattern represent transparent combinations of constructional and verbal semantics whereas others appear to owe nothing to the semantics which defines the productivity of the construction.

The claim that coverage is the prototypical implication of applicative sentences is supported not only by the frequency of this implication in the data set (see Appendix) but also by patterns of loss and innovation within the class of *be*-verbs over the last 200 years. For instance, a once sizeable class of verbs with removal semantics has lost all of its members, with the exception of the idiomatic verbs of theft discussed earlier. No new removal verbs have been innovated outside of the small theft subclass. By contrast, *be*-verbs with concrete coverage meanings have been innovated in great number (e.g., *bespiken* ‘put spikes onto [e.g. tires of moto-cross bikes]’; *bestrahlen* ‘illuminate; irradiate [e.g. food]’; *beampeln* ‘put up traffic lights [e.g., at intersections]’). Although the coverage class has lost members as well, these losses are piecemeal and appear to be due to lexical obsolescence (e.g., *beleitern* ‘put ladders down mining shafts [for access]’; *bezetteln* ‘put little pieces of paper on [as labels]’; *belehnen* ‘invest with a fiefdom’; *befrohnen* ‘impose corvée on’).

5.5 Verb Classes and Partial Productivity

The problem at issue is identical to that faced by theorists who assume lexical-rule approaches: how does one account for the fact that there are limitations on the productive use of a given argument-structure pattern? Pinker's solution to this problem is to posit narrow verb classes which define the productivity of a given lexico-semantic rule. While the rule provides necessary conditions for its application, the narrowly defined verb classes provide sufficient conditions on the application of the rule.

In accordance with Goldberg (1995), we assume that argument-structure constructions like the ditransitive are linked in associative memory with semantically defined verb clusters of varying degrees of strength. Strength derives from the type frequency of a given semantic class. For example, Goldberg argues that the class of verbs of transfer (e.g., *send, mail*) and the class of verbs of creation (e.g., *paint, bake*) have high type frequency vis-à-vis the ditransitive construction, and ascribes the high productivity of these classes to this fact, in accordance with Bybee's (1985, 1995) model of the productivity of open schemas. Weak clusters for Goldberg are those with low type frequency, and these will accordingly attract few new members. For the ditransitive, Goldberg identifies the class of verbs of envying as a weak class (whose only members are presumably *envy* and *begrudge*), while in the present case such a class is represented by verbs of removal. These are limited in modern German to verbs of theft; no innovative forms which we found in our corpus study could be classified as belonging to the removal class. By contrast, the class of causative verbs of coverage is highly productive vis-à-vis the applicative pattern. Innovative forms like *behaaren* and *beschildern* attest to this productivity.

The narrowly defined verb classes reflect limitations on the uses to which the constructional semantics can be put. Therefore, description of the constructional semantics will necessarily entail a careful description of the verb classes. However, the verb classes cannot be said to CONSTITUTE the constructional semantics. The reason for this is that the classification of a given verb may in fact be determined by the manner in which that verb's semantics is reconciled with the constructional semantics. The verb *befahren* '*be*-drive' is a case in point. We saw that when the direct object denotes a two-dimensional location (like a lake), *befahren* belongs to the core class of verbs denoting coverage. By contrast, when the direct object denotes a one-dimensional location (like a roadway), *befahren* is most appropriately grouped with verbs denoting iterated activity (see examples (5.120-5.121). In other words, class membership will often be resolvable only by appeal to linguistic context, where the context in question is defined by the applicative construction and the semantic types of the arguments. The point here is similar to that often made in studies of verbal aspect (e.g., Dowty 1991, Foley and Van Valin 1984): aspectual classification relies on information from predicate-argument structure, and therefore aspectual classes are not appropriately described as verb classes.

5.6 Restrictions on Verb-Construction Integration

A potential objection to our analysis of the German applicative pattern is that by emphasizing the ability of a given construction to cause a given verb (or other open-class item) to be construed as a coverage predicate, we have given up a constrained account, in which verbs themselves, via their inherent semantics, determine whether or not they are compatible with the applicative pattern. For example, we argued in chapter 3 that although the verb *wachsen* 'grow' is not inherently a verb of coverage, it is compatible with coverage semantics, since growth can be construed as the MEANS by which a plant covers a surface, as in example (2.17): *Kletterpflanzen, die mit speziellen Haftorganen Wände oder andere Flächen direkt bewachsen* 'Self-climbers = climbing plants that directly *be*-grow walls or other surfaces with the help of special adhesive/sticky extremities'.

By arguing that the high-frequency verb classes must be in principle infinitely expansible (to incorporate the productivity of the construction), we appear to be assuming that any verb can be a verb of coverage when combined with the applicative pattern. If we in fact held this assumption, we could not account for the fact that, as Brinkmann points out (p. 191), causativizable verbs of motion like *wirbeln* 'whirl' do not have *be*-prefixed counterparts. Brinkmann observes that while *wirbeln* is compatible with a directed-motion pattern, as in (5.143a), it is ill formed when combined with the applicative pattern, as in (5.143b):

(5.143) a. Die Dachziegel **wirbelten auf** die Straße.
'The roofing tiles whirled onto the street.'
(=Brinkmann 16: 191)
b. *Die Dachziegel **bewirbelten** die Straße.
'The roofing tiles *be*-whirled the street.'
(=Brinkmann 16: 191)

In fact, as we will now attempt to show, the constructional model which we have outlined is highly compatible with the presumption that the inherent semantics of verbs will constrain their ability to combine with the applicative construction. In describing incompatibilities like that in (5.143), we will make reference to semantic facts, like the topological constraint on *be*-predications, which are also recognized by Brinkmann. However, as we have seen, our account differs from that of Brinkmann in assuming that the applicative pattern directly expresses a polysemous semantic schema, involving both literal and metaphorical uses. For Brinkmann, the applicative pattern has no inherent semantics, polysemous or otherwise. For this reason, as we will now suggest, our model provides a more principled account of positive exceptions within the restricted classes of verbs. The constructional model allows for greater and lesser degrees of fit between the semantics of a given situation radical (predicate-argument complex) and the semantics of the construction. The potential for a given combination of verb and applicative pattern is determined not only by convention but also by whether or not an interpreter can plausibly reconcile verbal and constructional semantics. This reconciliation procedure may involve not only the prototypical usage of the construction, but also extended uses, including metaphorical ones.

In the remainder of this section, we will make the relevant observations with respect to semantically defined verb classes, noting in each case how the particular class relates to the classes proposed by Brinkmann. We will discuss Brinkmann's explanations for the restrictions upon these classes, as well as her explanations for positive exceptions within the restricted classes.

5.6.1 Accompanied Motion Verbs

This class is identical to that proposed by Brinkmann, following Pinker (1989), on pp. 185-186. It includes *ziehen* 'pull' and *schieben* 'push'. These are verbs which, as Pinker observes, involve a continuous imposition of force by the agent. Brinkmann observes that examples like the following are ill formed:

(5.144) *Er **bezog** den Parkplatz mit den Einkaufswagen.
'He *be*-pulled the parking lot with shopping carts.' (=Brinkmann 3: 186)

However, as Brinkmann herself observes (p. 186), *ziehen* does have an applicative usage, as exemplified by:

(5.145) Message ID <32F08A60.5BFC@uni-tuebingen.de>
Bei der Bundeswehr gab es so ein paar Muttersöhnchen, die hatten noch NIE ein Bett **bezogen** oder ein Hemd gefaltet.
'In the (German) army we had a few mama's boys who had NEVER put sheets on (lit. *be*-pulled) a bed or folded up a shirt.'

Brinkmann points out that *beziehen* denotes an action in which 'the theme is extended by being pulled [. . . and is] applied to the goal bit by bit' (p. 186). Other examples involve coverage of a couch by upholstery, or reflexive coverage of the sky by clouds, as in *Der Himmel bezieht sich* 'The sky is clouding over'. Brinkmann's account of the contrast in (5.144-5.145) is based on her nonindividuation hypothesis (p. 203). As discussed in section 2.3.2, the general thrust of this principle is that a theme which receives oblique coding (or is omitted) denotes an undifferentiated quantity of stuff, whose depletion does not 'measure out' the event denoted by the applicative predication. Nonindividuation is possible only when a verb which otherwise assigns an incremental theme does not assign one because it receives a processual construal. Brinkmann here proposes that incrementality of the theme of the input verb is a necessary condition on applicative formation: 'When the theme is not incremental [...], a process reading of the verb does not result in an interpretation of the theme as nonindividuated and so will not obviate the need to express the theme syntactically' (p. 113).

With regard to *ziehen* in particular, Brinkmann argues (pp. 112-113) that it, like its English analog *pull*, does not take an incremental theme; in predications involving these verbs, the theme is not apportioned over the course of the event, but instead occupies different sublocations along the path that the event entails. For this reason, she argues, a definite NP combined with *pull* yields a telic reading only when combined with a directional PP, as in *They pulled the shopping carts into the ravine (in two hours).* The same holds true of German *ziehen*, whether an extensible theme (i.e., a cover) is involved or not: *Er zog die Einkaufswagen* 'He pulled the shopping carts' and *Er zog die Decke* 'He pulled/dragged the blanket' are equally incompatible with a reading in which the direct object denotes an incremental theme. Given this fact, we cannot easily attribute the contrast in (5.144-5.145) to a difference in the incrementality of the theme argument of the input. Neither usage of *ziehen* seems to involve an incremental theme. Instead, this contrast may merit a simple explanation: when one pulls a blanket over a bed, prior sublocations are occupied along with later ones. This is what expansion entails. When one pulls shopping carts over an area, prior sublocations are necessarily abandoned. All shopping carts may be at the periphery of the area, since there is no limit on how far any one of them can be displaced from the point of origin. Clearly, the expansion scenario is far more concordant with the coverage scene denoted by the applicative construction. Since, as we argued in section 5.3.2, the applicative construction is also associated with iteration, we have a plausible explanation for another usage of *beziehen*, discussed in that section. In this usage, *beziehen* denotes the periodic receipt of goods or income. While admittedly a learner could not predict that *beziehen* should refer either to bed making or to drawing a pension, these usages constitute principled positive exceptions.

5.6.2 Verbs of Inherent Directed Motion

This class is identical to the class of Directional Verbs proposed by Brinkmann (pp. 186-187). These verbs, which inherently denote direction, include *fallen* 'fall', *sinken* 'sink, lower', their causative counterparts, and invariant intransitives like *steigen* 'rise'. As shown in (5.146-5.147), verbs of this class are incompatible with the applicative pattern:

(5.146) *Die Begonien **befielen** die Straße.
'The begonias *be*-fell the street.' (=Brinkmann 4a:187)

(5.147) Die Begonien **fielen auf** die Straße.
'The begonias fell onto the street.' (=Brinkmann 4a:187)

Brinkmann says of verbs in this class that they 'inherently denote direction, which may be oriented either upward, downward or deictically (i.e., to or away from a place that must be contextually determined)' (p. 186). Brinkmann (p. 197) suggests that these verbs cannot combine with the applicative pattern because they express location inherently, and therefore do not allow expression of the goal argument as a core grammatical function. Instead, the goal must be expressed by an oblique. Since, in our terms, the applicative construction prohibits the location argument from receiving oblique expression, verb and construction cannot unify.

This explanation is somewhat unsatisfying because there is nothing in principle that would prevent a verb of inherent directed motion from taking a location argument as a direct object, as in the case of English *enter, descend,* and *exit* (mentioned by Brinkmann in fn. 3, p. 199). Further, there are exceptions to the restriction, as shown by the following examples, involving the verb *befallen:*[30]

(5.148) 1800573
Dabei gibt es Lebensmittel, die weitaus häufiger von den winzigen Mikroben **befallen** sind.
'But there are foods that are attacked (lit. *be*-fallen) even more often by these tiny microbes.'

[30] Brinkmann (p. 187) discusses a contrast involving the positive exception *besteigen* 'mount, climb'. She suggests that *steigen* may alternate because it is not merely a directed motion verb, but instead one that entails a particular manner of motion, clambering. This seems plausible in that *besteigen* often takes a direct object denoting a mountain, but it additionally takes direct objects denoting ferries, cars, platforms, elevators, roofs, horses and thrones. For this reason, we view *besteigen* as reflecting not coverage semantics but the archaic proximity semantics of the prefix (see section 5.4).

(5.149) 36962931
Als Premier mit der niedrigsten Popularitätsrate in diesem Jahrhundert (17 Prozent) wird er für all die Übel verantwortlich gemacht, die den zweisprachigen Wohlfahrtsstaat im Norden der USA seit Beginn der 90er Jahre **befallen** haben.
'As the prime minister with the lowest approval ratings in this century (17 percent) he is held responsible for all the evils that have befallen this bilingual welfare state to the north of the US since the beginning of the nineties.'

The verb *befallen* as used in (5.148-5.149) has both metonymic and metaphorical properties. In (5.148), the coverage semantics of the pattern combines with the verb's semantics to yield a reading of coverage by means of falling. Since this schema is prototypically entailed by an enemy attack, invoking it becomes a conventional way of denoting an attack. The predications in (5.148-5.149) are metaphorical in that the themes involved (microbes, evils) are nonagentive. The existence of a verb *befallen* with a metaphorical construal of this type cannot be predicted, but the meaning in question is far from opaque, since it combines verbal and constructional semantics via the means relation (falling is the means by which coverage is effected).

5.6.3 Verbs of Nondirected Motion

This class is identical to Brinkmann's subclass of Causativizable Verbs of Motion (pp. 191-192). Among the verbs in this class are *wirbeln* 'whirl' and *rollen* 'roll'. A grammaticality contrast involving *wirbeln* was given in (5.143a-b). Brinkmann illustrates this constraint for *rollen* with examples like **Er berollt den Billardtisch mit Kugeln* 'He *be*-rolls the billiard table with balls' (p. 204). Brinkmann's explanation of the behavior of this class is based upon Wunderlich's (1992) satisfaction criteria for the locative alternation (discussed in section 2.3.1). In that section and in section 3.6, we argued for a construction-based construal of this principle rather than one based upon Löbner's Presupposition of Indivisibility (1990). However, both Brinkmann's analysis and our analysis require that the theme argument of a *be*-predication be construed as occupying a salient number of subregions within the location (whether sequentially or summarily). Brinkmann suggests that this interpretive feature of *be*-predications can be used to explain the restrictions upon this class if one makes the additional assumption that the subregions of the location 'may not be ordered in any particular way' (p. 200). Verbs of the *rollen* class are said to violate this constraint, for the following reason:

> These verbs denote uncontrolled motion. An entity that moves without control, e.g., a ball rolling down a street, is subject to the physical forces impinging on it, i.e., it cannot change the direction of its motion. This means that the various subregions of the street over which the ball is rolling are not reached in an arbitrary order; rather their order is determined by the physical forces impinging on the ball. (ibid)

This explanation is problematic from our perspective, since there does not appear to be any reason in principle that coverage of a surface cannot be achieved through traversal of an ordered series of subregions. Applicative verbs like *besticken* 'embroider' clearly entail an ordered series of subregions, as in *Sie bestickte das Tischtuch mit feinen Mustern* 'She embroidered (lit. *be*-stuck) the tablecloth with fine patterns'. And in fact, controlled rolling appears far more compatible with coverage than uncontrolled rolling: in the case of an agent rolling balls around a billiard table, it is difficult to achieve a construal in which the balls simultaneously occupy the table's surface rather than the periphery of the table. When the scene depicted involves controlled rolling, as when rolling is a means of locomotion, a coverage construal is readily achieved. This is the case in the applicative example given in (5.150):

(5.150) Message ID <199804070905.a28261@whv.maus.de>
Rollstuhlfahrer Poul Schacksen aus Kopenhagen will den 1997 erschienenen Wegweiser Handiguide Europa fortführen und zusammen mit Movado Berlin **berollen**. Der Däne hat zusammen mit Behindertenvereinen Informationen für mobilitätseingeschränkte Touristen gesammelt und in der ersten Publikation Rom, Prag, Paris, London, Kopenhagen und Stockholm vorgestellt.
'Wheelchair user Poul Schacksen of Copenhagen wants to continue the guide 'Handiguide Europe', which came out in 1997, and *be*-roll Berlin together with Movado. The Dane has collected information for mobility-impaired tourists with the help of organizations of handicapped people. The first publication presented Rome, Prague, London, Copenhagen, and Stockholm.'

In (5.150), *berollen* appears synonymous with *befahren* '*be*-drive'. This example suggests again that restrictions upon applicative formation are best stated at the level of predicate-argument structure rather than at the level of the verb.

5.6.4 Verbs of Surface Depression

This class subsumes three classes proposed by Brinkmann: PRESS verbs, STIR verbs and INTO verbs. Verbs of this class denote actions in which an interior region is either created or acted upon. Verbs which belong to this class are *füllen* 'fill', *schütten* 'pour', *stopfen* 'stuff', *rühren* 'stir', *kneten* 'knead', *drücken* 'press/push', *pressen* 'press' and *klopfen* 'beat/knock'. Brinkmann explains the failure of STIR and PRESS verbs to participate in the locative alternation in terms of the nonindividuation hypothesis, by which the input verb must assign an incremental theme (see section 2.3.2). As Brinkmann points out, verbs like *kneten* and *drücken* lack the thematic structure necessary to permit nonsyntactic expression of the theme; they are not transfer verbs. By contrast, INTO verbs typically are transfer verbs which assign incremental themes (e.g., if one pours water into a cup, the depletion of the water in the pitcher 'measures out' the event). Brinkmann explains the failure of INTO verbs to undergo the locative alternation by the constraint that the location must be conceived of as a surface (p. 205).

The nonindividuation hypothesis is highly problematic as a potential explanation for the restrictions upon STIR and PRESS verbs. As we saw in section 2.3.2, this principle is relativized to trivalent verbs of transfer, since it is only transfer verbs which permit deindividuation of the theme argument. The verbs in the STIR and PRESS class are bivalent verbs, none of which denote transfer inherently. In her examples, Brinkmann places these verbs in trivalent frames (pp. 187-189), but here the caused-motion implication comes not from the verb semantics but from the addition of the directional adverbial. Therefore, the nonindividuation hypothesis cannot be a candidate explanation for the behavior of these classes. However, in basic accordance with Brinkmann (p. 205), we assume that the general failure of INTO verbs to combine with the applicative pattern is due to a topological constraint which we view as a semantic feature of the applicative construction: the location must be a two-dimensional surface and therefore cannot have depth. As we have observed, there are positive exceptions within the INTO class. One such exception involves the verb *füllen*, which, we showed above, does have an applicative counterpart, *befüllen*. Brinkmann, mentioning this exception, chooses to overlook it as a 'baroque coinage' which 'is not accepted by all speakers' (p. 185). However, our corpus data provide highly idiomatic examples of *befüllen*. Two such examples, given as (3.78-3.79) above are repeated here as (5.151-5.152):

(5.151) *Frankfurter Allgemeine Zeitung*, August 7, 1990
Außerdem müßten Betriebe, die Mehrwegflaschen **befüllen**, eine plötzliche Erhöhung ihrer Pfandrückstellungen bewältigen.
'Moreover companies that *be*-fill returnable bottles would have to cope with suddenly having to raise their reserve for deposits.'

(5.152) *Süddeutsche Zeitung*, July 25, 1994
Darüber hinaus werden im Jemen 5 Milliarden US-Dollar für eine Erdgas-Verflüssigungsanlage bei Aden oder Mukalla fällig, um dort die Tanker nach Japan zu **befüllen**.
'Moreover 5 billion US dollars will become due for a natural gas liquefaction plant near Aden or Mukalla that serves to *be*-fill the tankers bound for Japan.'

Each of these examples involves a predicate-argument structure which is compatible with the semantics of the applicative construction. As observed in section 3.5, these examples have iterative readings, in which the bottles or tankers are repeatedly filled. It was suggested in that section that the space-time coordinates of the individual filling events can be viewed as collectively defining a surface over which coverage is effected. Since we allow that the applicative construction can entail iteration without the coverage implication, these predications might also be said to express iterated action alone. In either case, these examples show that the event type denoted by *füllen* may be construed as compatible with the constructional semantics, as per the override principle given in section 3.1. A similar point is made by examples like (5.153):

(5.153) www.schulefriesgasse.ac.at/vs/
Die Kinder bauen einen 2x2x2 m großen Berg und **beschütten** ihn mit Farbe.
'The children build a hill of 2x2x2 meters and *be*-pour it with paint.'

In this example, we see that another INTO verb, *schütten*, can be reconstrued as a 'surface' verb when combined with the applicative construction. Rather than denoting iterated pouring, the predication denotes an act in which paint saturates (i.e., covers) the surface of the hill. Principled exceptional behavior is also seen among verbs of pressing like *drücken*. Brinkmann points out (p. 188) that an applicative form of this verb does occur, as in *Er bedrückte den Knopf* 'He *be*-pressed the button', although trivalent examples denoting transfer appear infelicitous. Brinkmann observes that *bedrücken* 'specifies that an object is pressed repeatedly'. If this is the case (our native-speaker consultants did not have such a reading for *bedrücken*), there appears to be no motivation for this fact on Brinkmann's account; there is no general pragmatic principle by which an implication of iteration would attach to verbs derived via preposition incorporation. On the present account, iteration is a semantic value conventionally attached to the applicative construction. A verb which does not otherwise have an iterative construal may receive one in combination with the construction. Principled exceptions within this class are not limited to the iteration cases described by Brinkmann. The verb *bedrücken* also a metaphorical construal, which is compositionally related to the affectedness implication of the construction:

(5.154) Die Nachricht **bedrückte** ihn.
'The news depressed (lit. *be*-pressed) him.'

Positive exceptions within the PRESS class may also involve the literal semantics of the applicative construction, as in following example, involving the verb *klopfen* 'beat, knock':

(5.155) Message ID <6zji7FI802B@frosch.seerose.kristall.de>
Die Eier rundherum vorsichtig mit einem Löffel **beklopfen**, bis die Schale von einem Netzwerk feiner Risse bedeckt ist.
'*Be*-knock the eggs all around carefully with a spoon, until the shell is covered by a network of fine fissures.'

The meaning of the novel applicative token in (5.154) is compositionally related to coverage semantics via the means relation: knocking is the means by which coverage of the surface is effected. The same general point about constructional meaning can be made with regard to the STIR class. Brinkmann describes positive exceptions within this class involving intensive readings of verbs of mixing and stirring (p. 189). Since on our account the applicative construction denotes intensive action, these exceptions can be treated as reconciliation effects. Under Brinkmann's assumptions, these *be*-prefixed forms must simply be treated as lexical exceptions; their meanings have nothing to do with the complex of meanings associated with the applicative pattern.

5.6.5 Verbs of Position

This class is identical to Brinkmann's Causativizable Verbs of Position (pp. 189-190). This class includes verbs with identical transitive and causative forms, e.g., *stecken* 'stick', *hängen* 'hang', and *lehnen* 'lean'. It also includes verb pairs like *sitzen/setzen* 'sit/set', *stehen/stellen* 'stand/ put', and *liegen/legen* 'lie/lay'. This class is a problematic example of a nonalternating class, since, as Brinkmann points out, almost every verb listed does in fact have an applicative counterpart. This therefore appears to be a class built entirely of exceptions. However, many of the applicative verbs found in this class have idiosyncratic interpretations, i.e., meanings in which the verb does not obviously have a means relation to the event type denoted by the construction. For example, causative *setzen* does not have a causative meaning in the applicative pattern in examples like (2.36), repeated here as (5.156) :

(5.156) 5939806
Am Wochenende mußten 7000 Heilsuchende davon abgehalten werden, Nachbargrundstücke zu **besetzen** und Straßen zu blockieren.
'On the weekend 7000 patients had to be prevented from occupying (lit. *be*-setting) neighboring properties and from blocking streets.'

In (5.156), *besetzen* is used to denote the coverage of an area by means of sitting, although the base verb, *setzen*, does not mean 'sit', but 'set'. While there is an applicative form of *sitzen* 'sit', this form means not 'cover a surface by sitting' but 'own' (as in *Ich besizte einen Toaster* 'I own a toaster'). This meaning of *besitzen* may have developed from an earlier, transparent Middle High German meaning for *besitzen*, 'occupy', via the association between occupation and ownership of land. This development may have caused *besetzen* to attract the earlier meaning of *besitzen* in addition to its causative meaning. As Brinkmann observes (p. 190), *besetzen* is used with a coverage implication in examples like *Sie besetzte die Jacke mit Perlen* (lit. 'She *be*-set the jacket with pearls'). Brinkmann claims (p. 190) that this usage of *besetzen* is idiosyncratic, because it does not entail that the theme attains the body posture associated with sitting. We do not view this argument as persuasive, however, since the verb *setzen*, like the English verb *set*, does not entail attainment of this body posture either. The case of *belegen* '*be*-lay' is similar to that of *besetzen*. *Belegen* has both causative and noncausative uses. As a causative, *belegen* can mean 'top [as with an open-faced sandwich]'; as a noncausative, *belegen* means 'occupy'. However, *beliegen* '*be*-lie', unlike *besitzen* '*be*-sit', has a compositional usage, shown in (5.157):

(5.157) Message ID <slrn7m9pjg.1ri.neko@sleepy.space.net>
Sag ihr, dass ihre Katze pro Tag *mindestens* eine Stunde intensive Betreuung (Spielen/Schmusen) verlangt, sowie regelmässige erzieherische Aufmerksamkeit (Kratzbaum mit Nachdruck zum Kratzen nehmen lassen, nix anderes, Tische erklettern, Betten **beliegen** [...]).
'Tell her that her cat requires *at least* an hour of intensive looking after (playing/cuddling) a day as well as regular attention to training (enforce the use of scratching posts—nothing else; [prevent] climbing up onto tables, *be*-lying of beds [...]).'

Thus, despite idiosyncratic behavior within this class of verbs, there is a good deal that is transparent from our perspective, and Brinkmann observes that the verbs of position provide 'the best example to demonstrate the role of contextual conditions' (p. 207). She postulates that these verbs are compatible with the applicative pattern insofar as they denote a type of attachment and the goal 'can be conceived as a surface' (p. 207).[31] She argues that this latter condition, which is identical to our planar-surface condition, is responsible for differences in acceptability involving different predicate-argument structures for verbs like *hängen*, as in the following examples:

(5.158) a. Sie **behängte** die Wand mit Bildern.
'She *be*-hung the wall with pictures.'
b. ??Sie **behängte** die Wäschleine mit Handtüchern.
'She *be*-hung the clothesline with handtowels.

Brinkmann points out that since the clothesline in (5.158b) is a one-dimensional location, the planar surface constraint on applicatives is violated, resulting in unacceptability. This observation is of course entirely consistent with our general point in this section: that situation type as expressed in predicate-argument structure can influence the acceptability of a given applicative predication. While one cannot ignore lexical idiosyncrasy, the existence of contrasts like that found in (5.158) strongly suggests that interpreters make judgments about the degree of fit between the situation denoted by the particular predicate-argument combination and that denoted by the construction. In our analysis, the planar-location constraint is part of the signification of the applicative construction. On Brinkmann's account, as described in section 2.3.3., this constraint is imposed by the bound prefix *be*. As we argued in that section, these two accounts amount to the same thing: if the existence of a given lexical entry is contingent upon the existence of a given construction, then it is impossible to discern the difference between the semantic constraints of that lexical entry and those of the construction.

In sum, while the semantic constraints associated with verb classes are good indicators of the ability of a given verb within that class to combine with the applicative construction, the apparently exceptional behavior of certain verbs within these classes makes sense only if one looks at predicate-argument structure (rather than verb meaning alone)

---

[31] In this section Brinkmann proposes a new topological condition on *be*-prefixation: that the theme be conceived of as a point (p. 207). We do not see how this condition could be a general condition on applicative formation, since it is violated in some of the most straightforward trivalent examples given by Brinkmann, including *beladen* '*be*-load', *bespritzen*, '*be*-spritz', *bemalen* '*be*-paint', and *beschmieren* '*be*-smear'.

and the effect of constructional meaning upon the construal of an event type. Since the applicative construction is polysemous, the semantic reconciliation procedure assumed involves the same interpretive latitude that characterizes many of the attested examples.

Conclusion

We have sought to establish that the German applicative pattern should be described as a symbolic unit rather than as the product of a lexical rule. By examining constraints and effects which are directly attributable to the *be*-pattern (valence creation and augmentation, holistic and planar interpretation of the location argument, omissibility of the theme argument), we have suggested that this argument-structure pattern does something that only verbs are generally thought to do: denote an event type. Since a syntactic construction can mean what it means in the way that a word means what it means—via convention—it makes sense that an argument-structure pattern should, like a polysemous word, denote an associative network of senses; we have discussed the prototype-based semantics of coverage associated with the *be*-pattern. Along with Bybee et al. (1994), we adopt the view that the semantic substance associated with a given formative is the accretion of a series of diachronic developments. Like these authors, we see the diachronic dimension as greatly increasing the explanatory power of semantic theory. As they point out, one cannot explain the existence of a particular construction by showing that it has a particular function or functions; one must also explain how that construction developed its functions (p. 3). Describing the relevant patterns of semantic extension is a coherent enterprise only if one assumes a sign-based semantics for constructions. In accordance with Goldberg (1995), we maintain that to admit 'top down' or syntactic meaning does not conflict with the goal of providing a compositional theory of sentence semantics: on the constructional account, sentence interpretation is a procedure by which the situation type denoted by a predicate-argument complex is related to the situation type denoted by the construction.

Appendix: Verb Classes

Following is a listing of the verbs that we took into consideration for our analysis. It cannot be complete, since *be-* is productive. It does not include verbs that we could not find attested in contemporary use or that neither we nor our consultants were able to use with confidence. The verb classes appear in the order in which they were discussed in chapter 5 of the paper. Section 1 contains the verbs exemplifying the central coverage scenario. Section 2 lists the verbs whose meanings represent metaphorical extensions of the central sense. Section 3 lists verbs whose meanings involve pragmatic inference. We also list verbs that exemplify marginally productive or unproductive subclasses: the historically primary SURROUNDING sense (section 4), the REMOVAL sense (section 5), the PROXIMITY sense (section 6), ornative pseudo *be*-PARTICIPLES (section 7). In the final section, section 8, we list verbs that could not be assigned to any of our classes because the source is morphologically opaque and/or because the synchronic meanings of the source word and the *be*-verb do not relate in any of the ways we discuss. Notice, however, that many of these words could be assigned to classes if historical data were taken into account. For instance, *begehren* 'desire' which is opaque to speakers today is historically a denominal form from the source nominal *ger* 'desire', similar to the transparent *beneiden* 'envy', which we assign to the class 'Attending to a percept as contact with it'. By the same token, a verb that is listed in a certain class may historically have been more representative of another sense. *Bestürzen* 'dismay, shock', for instance, is listed in the affectedness section but earlier meant 'topple over, put on its head' with *be-* contributing a notion of rotation that is expressed by *be-*'s historical twin, the prefix *um* 'around', in Modern German. The order of presentation is not intended to reflect the relative chronology of the development of the senses. Nor are the classes mutually exclusive. For instance, *bewerfen* '*be*-throw, pelt' is listed in the iteration section even though it might also be grouped with verbs of intensive action, since repeated pelting of a target with projectiles can be said to involve greater intensity than a single act of throwing. Within a class, the *be*-verbs are given in alphabetical order. Each *be*-verb is followed by parentheses containing, respectively: a gloss for the source word and a gloss for the *be*-verb, with the two glosses separated by a diamond symbol (◇). In cases in which the part of speech of the source word cannot be determined, we star the English word to the left of the diamond if it is ambiguous between the candidate parts of speech, usually verb and noun. If there is no single word to capture the part of speech ambiguity that exists in German, we give English glosses for the candidate parts of speech, separated by a slash /. If the *be*-verb is morphologically opaque (and thus in the class of unassigned verbs), only its idiomatic gloss will be listed.

1 The Coverage Scenario

1.1 Bivalent[Theme Covers Location]

bedrücken	to weigh down ◇ depress
befallen	to fall ◇ strike down, seize, infest
befahren	to move, drive ◇ move, drive around [area]
befingern	finger ◇ finger
befühlen	feel ◇ feel
befummeln	to fiddle around, fumble around ◇finger, touch
begrapschen	grab ◇ grab at
begehen	to walk, go ◇ inspect, take a walking tour around
beglänzen	to shine ◇ shine on
begrasen	to graze ◇ graze on
begreifen	grab◇ grab, grasp on
behängen	to hang ◇ hang all over
beklettern	to climb ◇ climb around on
bekrabbeln	to crawl ◇ crawl around on
bekriechen	to creep ◇ creep around on
belecken	to lick ◇ lick over
belegen	to lie on ◇ occupy
beleuchten	to glow ◇ glow, shine on
bemannen	man ◇ staff, run, man
bepilgern	to go on a pilgrimage to ◇ peregrinate

beradeln	to bike ◇ bike around in
bereisen	to travel ◇ travel around in, tour
beriechen	to smell, sniff ◇ smell, sniff around
berollen	to roll ◇ roll all over [e.g., in a wheel chair]
berudern	to row ◇ row around on
beschatten	shade ◇ shade [place]; shadow [person]
bescheinen	to shine ◇ shine on
beschnüffeln	to smell, sniff ◇ smell, sniff around
beschnuppern	to smell, sniff ◇ smell, sniff around
besegeln	to sail ◇ sail around on
besetzen	to set ◇ occupy
besiedeln	to settle ◇ settle in, populate
besitzen	to sit on ◇ possess
bespannen	to span ◇ span, stretch over
bespielen	to play ◇ play on [pitch, sports ground]
bespringen	to jump ◇ jump around on
bespritzen	to stand ◇ [e.g. trees] stand all over
betasten	to grope ◇ touch, feel
betatschen	to paw ◇ grope
bevölkern	people ◇ populate
bewachsen	to grow ◇ grow all over
bewandern	to hike ◇ hike around
beweiden	to graze ◇ graze on
bewohnen	to live ◇ inhabit
bewuchern	to grow rampant ◇ grow rampant all over
beziehen	to pull ◇ make up [a bed]

1.2 Trivalent [Agent Covers Location with Theme]

beatmen	breath ◇ give artificial respiration
beampeln	traffic light ◇ equip with [traffic lights]
bebauen	build on ◇ cover with [buildings]
bebildern	picture ◇ illustrate with [pictures]
bedachen	roof ◇ cover [house] with [roof]
bedampfen	steam ◇ expose to [steam]; cover with [material in steam form]
bedecken	to put on, over ◇ cover with
bedrecken	dirt ◇ soil with

bedrucken	to print on ◇ print with
beduften	scent ◇ perfume with
beflaggen	flag ◇ decorate with [flags]
beflecken	stain ◇ soil with
beflicken	to mend, sew ◇ sew with
befrachten	freight ◇ load with
befruchten	fruit ◇ fertilize, pollinate [e.g. plant] with [seed]
begaben	gift, talent ◇endow with [talents]
begasen	gas ◇ expose to [gas]
beglänzen	to glow ◇ shine on
behaaren	hair ◇ cover with [hair]
behängen	to hang on ◇ hang with
beimpfen	to vaccinate ◇ vaccinate [culture medium] with [bacteria]
behäufeln	to heap up ◇ cover [location] by heap-ing up
behauchen	to breathe ◇ breathe at with
behufen	horseshoe ◇ put hooves on [horse]
bekacken	shit* ◇ shit
bekiesen	gravel ◇ cover with [gravel]
bekleckern	spill, dribble on ◇ spill with
beklecksen	spill, dribble on ◇ stain with
bekleiden	dress* ◇ dress with
bekleistern	glue ◇ cover with [sticky substance]
beköstigen	food ◇ feed with
bekohlen	coal ◇ provide with [coal]
bekotzen	to vomit ◇ vomit with
bekränzen	garland, wreath/to crown with ◇ crown with
bekreuzen, sich	cross ◇ make the sign of the cross
bekreuzigen, sich	cross ◇ make the sign of the cross
bekritzeln	to scribble on ◇ scribble with
beladen	to load on ◇ load with
belauben,sich	foliage ◇ cover self with [leaves]
belegen	to lay on ◇ cover with
belehnen	fief ◇ provide with [fief]
beleimen	glue ◇ cover with [glue]

beleimen	glue ◇ cover [location] by gluing on [theme]
beleuchten	to shine ◇ illuminate with
belichten	light ◇ expose [film] to [light, flash]
beliefern	to deliver to ◇ supply with
belohnen	reward* ◇ reward with
bemalen	to paint on ◇ paint with
bemannen	man ◇ man, staff [workplace] with [people]
bemessern	knife ◇ equip with [knives/blades]
benageln	to nail on ◇ nail with
benähen	to sew on ◇ sew with
benässen	to wet/wetness ◇ wet, moisten with
benetzen	wet, moisten ◇ moisten; sprinkle with
bepacken	to pack into, on ◇ pack with
bepanzern	armor-plate* ◇ armor-plate with
bepflanzen	to plant on ◇ plant with
bepflastern	pavement/pave ◇ pave with
bepflastern	medical plaster ◇ cover with [plaster]
bepinkeln	to piss ◇ piss with
bepinseln	to paint on◇ paint with
bepissen	to piss ◇ piss with
beregnen	to rain ◇ spray with
bereifen	tire ◇ equip with [tires]
berieseln	to trickle on ◇ trickle with
beringen	ring ◇ equip [e.g. birds] with [type of ring]
berußen	soot ◇ cover with [soot]
besabbern	to dribble ◇ slobber, dribble with
besäen	to sow on ◇ sprinkle with; sow [field] with
besaiten	string ◇ string with
besamen	semen ◇ inseminate, pollinate with
besanden	sand ◇ cover with sand
bescheinen	to shine ◇ shine on, light up with
bescheissen	to shit* ◇ shit with
beschenken	to give to ◇ present with
beschichten	layer, coat ◇ coat with
beschicken	to send to ◇ load, charge with

beschiffen	to piss ◇ piss with
beschildern	traffic signs ◇ equip with [traffic signs]
beschlagen	to hit ◇ cover with; shoe [e.g. a horse]
beschmieren	to smear on ◇ smear with
beschmutzen	dirt ◇ soil with
beschneien	to snow ◇ cover with [artificial snow]
beschottern	gravel ◇ cover with [gravel]
beschreiben	to write on ◇ cover with [writing]
beschriften	writing ◇ label with
beschuhen	shoe ◇ shoe with [e.g. a metal tip]
beschütten	to spill on ◇ spill with
besetzen	to set on ◇ occupy with
besiedeln	to settle at, on ◇ settle [location] with [people]
besiegeln	seal* ◇ seal [document] with a seal; confirm, seal with
besingen	to sing on ◇ record [a medium] with [songs]
besohlen	sole ◇ sole with [type of sole]
besolden	soldier's pay ◇ pay [soldiers; state officials] with
bespannen	span over ◇ span with
bespeien	to vomit ◇ vomit with
bespicken	to lard with ◇ lard with
bespielen	to play on ◇ record [medium] with [data]
bespiken	spike ◇ equip [tires] with spikes
besprechen	to speak on ◇ record [medium] with [speech]
besprengen	sprinkle, spray on ◇ sprinkle with
besprenkeln	sprinkle, spray on ◇ sprinkle with
besprinkeln	sprinkle, spray on ◇ sprinkle with
bespritzen	to splash on ◇ splash with
besprühen	spray on ◇ spray with
bespucken	to spit on ◇ spit with
bestäuben	dust ◇ dust, spray with
bestecken	stick on ◇ cover by sticking on
besticken	embroider on ◇ embroider with
bestrahlen	ray ◇ irradiate with
bestreichen	to spread on ◇ spread with

bestreuen	to strew on ◇ strew with
bestücken	piece ◇ equip, arm with
bestuhlen	chair ◇ equip with [seats]
besudeln	to spill on ◇ stain with
betexten	write words ◇ write words, lyrics to [e.g. piece of music]
beträufeln	to trickle on ◇ trickle with
betropfen	to drip, trickle on ◇ trickle with
betröpfeln	to dribble, trickle on ◇ trickle with
betupfen	to dab on ◇ dab with
bevölkern	people ◇ populate with
bevorschussen	advance ◇ provide with [sum] as an advance
bewaffnen	weapon ◇ arm with
bewässern	to water ◇ irrigate
beweiden	to graze ◇ make [animals] graze on
bewölken, sich	cloud ◇ cloud over, become overcast
bewurzeln, sich	root ◇ take roots
beziehen	put on ◇ cover with
bezuschussen	grant ◇ subsidize with [amount]

2 Metaphorical Extensions

2.1 Discourse as Travel across a Topic

bedichten	to write poetry ◇ write poetry on
beflüstern	to whisper ◇ whisper about
begähnen	to yawn ◇ yawn over
begrinsen	to grin ◇ grin over
beheulen	to cry ◇ cry over
behupen	to honk a horn ◇ honk a horn over
bejammern	to moan ◇ moan over
bejodeln	to yodel ◇ yodel over
bejohlen	to bawl, yell ◇ bawl, yell over
bejubeln	to cheer ◇ cheer over
bekichern	to snicker ◇ snicker over
beklagen	to complain ◇ complain about
beklatschen	to clap ◇ applaud, clap over
beklatschen	to gossip ◇ gossip about
beklönen	to chatter ◇ chatter about

bekrähen	to crow ◇ crow over
bekritteln	to criticize ◇ criticize
belächeln	to smile ◇ smile over
belachen	to laugh ◇ laugh at, over
bemäkeln	find fault ◇ criticize [that], find fault with [a situation, thing]
bemeckern	to bleat ◇ bleat over
bequasseln	to yak away ◇ gossip about
bequatschen	to gossip ◇ talk, gossip about
beratschen	to gossip ◇ gossip about
bereden	to talk ◇ talk about, discuss
besabbeln	to drivel ◇ gossip about
besabbern	to dribble, slaver ◇ gossip, talk about
beschmunzeln	to smile ◇ smile over
beschnacken	to chat ◇ chat about
beschreiben	to write ◇ write about, describe
beschreien	to cry ◇ conjure up [an event]
beschwafeln	to waffle ◇ waffle on, go on about
beschwatzen	to chat ◇ chat about
beschwören	to swear ◇ swear to
beseufzen	to sigh ◇ sigh over
besingen	to sing ◇ sing about
bespötteln	to mock, gibe ◇ make fun of
bespotten	to make fun ◇ make fun of
besprechen	to talk ◇ talk over
bestreiten	to argue about ◇ contest, dispute, challenge
betratschen	to gossip ◇ gossip about
beweinen	to cry ◇ cry over
bewiehern	to whinny ◇ whinny over
bewinseln	to whine ◇ whine over
bewitzeln	to make jokes ◇ make jokes about

2.2 Seeing as Contact with the Percept

beaufsichtigen	supervision ◇ supervise
beaugapfeln	apple of one's eye ◇ watch closely
beäugen	eyes ◇ have a good look at
beaugenscheinigen	field of vision ◇ examine
begaffen	to gape ◇ gape at
beglotzen	to gawk ◇ gawk at
begucken	to look ◇ have a good look at
behorchen	to listen ◇ listen in on
belauschen	to listen ◇ listen in on
beschauen	to look ◇ examine, inspect
besehen	to see, look ◇ have a look at, examine
besichtigen	view, vision ◇ tour, view, visit
bestaunen	to be amazed at ◇ admire, stare at

2.3 Attending to a Percept as Contact with it

beabsichtigen	intention ◇ intend
beachten	to pay attention to ◇ follow, obey; notice
beackern	to plow ◇ work through, on [topics]
bearbeiten	to work ◇ work on, deal with
beargwöhnen	suspicion, mistrust ◇ be suspicious of
bebrüten	to brood ◇ brood over
bedenken	to think ◇ ponder, consider
befolgen	to follow, succeed ◇ follow, heed, comply with [rules]
beforschen	to research ◇ do research on
beherzigen	heart ◇ heed, follow [advice]
behüten	to guard, protect, watch over ◇ protect, watch over
belauern	to lie in wait; lurk ◇ lie in wait for; spy on
bemerken	to feel, sense ◇ notice; realize;
bemitleiden	pity, sympathy ◇ pity
beneiden	envy* ◇ envy
beobachten	attention ◇ watch, observe
bereuen	regret ◇ regret [past action]
berücksichtigen	consideration ◇ consider
beschirmen	to guard ◇ guard

beschlafen	to sleep ◇ sleep over [a decision]
beschnarchen	to snore ◇ spend time snoring over [a decision]
beschützen	to guard ◇ protect
besinnen, sich	to reflect, think ◇ reflect, think about [*topic]
besorgen	care, concern ◇ look after; get, provide
betrachten	pursuit, striving ◇ look at
betrauern	to mourn ◇ mourn over
betreuen	faithful, loyal/faithfulness, loyalty ◇ look after, see to; coach
bewachen	to watch over, keep an eye on ◇ watch over, guard
bewahren	to maintain, preserve; look after ◇ preserve, protect
bewundern	wonder ◇ admire
bezwecken	purpose ◇ aim at bringing about, have in mind
bezweifeln	doubt* ◇ doubt, question

3 Inference-based Extensions

3.1 Extensions Based on the Transfer Entailment

Affecting as transfer

beeinflussen	influence ◇ influence
beenden	end* ◇ end, finish
beengen	narrow ◇ make narrow
befähigen	capable ◇ enable
befehden	feud ◇have a feud with, be hostile towards
befestigen	fast, firm, solid ◇ fortify [location]; attach [theme] to [location]
befeuchten	moist ◇ moisten
beflügeln	wing ◇ inspire
befreien	free ◇ free
befremden	unfamiliar ◇ estrange
befrieden	peace ◇ bring peace to
befriedigen	peace ◇ satisfy
befristen	deadline ◇ set a time limit

begeifern	dribble*, slaver* ◇ attack, harass verbally
beglaubigen	belief, credit ◇ authenticate, certify
beglücken	luck, happiness ◇ make happy, delight
begradigen	straight ◇ straighten out
begeistern	spirit ◇ inspire
begnaden	grace ◇ endow with
begnadigen	grace ◇ pardon
begrünen	green ◇ plant with [vegetation]
begünstigen	favor ◇ favor, further
begütigen	good, kind ◇ placate, appease
begutachten	examination ◇ give an opinion on
beirren	confused ◇ disconcert, put off
beklagen	complain/complaint ◇ sue
bekriegen	war ◇ wage war against
beleben	life ◇ enliven animate
beleidigen	harm ◇ insult, offend
beleihen	to lend ◇ take a mortgage out on
belustigen	funny, amusing, merry ◇ entertain
bekunden	known ◇ announce, make known
bemächtigen, sich	powerful ◇ take possession of
bemängeln	defect, lack ◇ criticize [that], find fault with [a situation, thing]
benoten	grade ◇ assign a grade to [a performance, schoolwork]
benötigen	necessary ◇ require, need
berauschen	intoxication ◇ intoxicate
berechtigen	right ◇ entitle, give the right
bereichern	rich ◇ make richer, enrich
bereinigen	clean ◇ clear up, settle
berichtigen	correct, true ◇ correct
beruhigen	calm ◇ calm down
besänftigen	soft, calm ◇ appease
beschleunigen	speedy ◇ speed up
beschönigen	beautiful ◇ gloss over
beschuldigen	guilt ◇ blame
beschulen	school ◇ provide with instruction
beschweren	heavy ◇ weigh down

beschwingen	wing ◇ cheer, elate
beseelen	soul ◇ inspire, buoy up
beseligen	overjoyed ◇ make happy, fill with bliss
bestärken	strength ◇ strengthen
bestätigen	constant, steady ◇ confirm
bestreiken	to strike ◇ strike against [company]
betätigen	active ◇ set in motion
betäuben	numb, deaf ◇ deafen, anesthetize
betiteln	title ◇ give [book] [title]; address [person] with [title]
betören	fool ◇ beguile, turn somebody's head
betrüben	sad ◇ sadden
beunruhigen	restless ◇ worry
beurkunden	document, record, diploma ◇ record; certify, authenticate; register [births]
beurlauben	vacation, leave ◇ suspend; give time off
beurteilen	to give one's opinion ◇ judge
bevollmächtigen	authorization ◇ authorize
bevorrechten	privilege ◇ grant privileges to
bevorrechtigen	privilege ◇ grant privileges to
bevorteilen	advantage ◇ favor
bevorzugen	priority, advantage, preference◇ prefer; give preferential treatment; give priority
bewerten	value* ◇ evaluate, attach a value to
bezähmen	to tame/tame ◇ make tame; curb, restrain
bezaubern	charm, spell ◇ cast a spell on

Communication as Transfer

beanspruchen	claim ◇ lay claim to
beanstanden	offense ◇ complain about; criticize
beantragen	motion ◇ move, propose
beantworten	answer ◇ reply to [a question]
beauftragen	assignment ◇ commission to do, put in charge of
befürworten	support ◇ back, recommend
beglückwünschen	congratulations ◇ congratulate

begrüßen	greet, say hello ◇ welcome [a person]; welcome, applaud [an event, a development]
bejahen	yes ◇ answer yes to [question]; see positively
beloben	laud ◇ praise, commend
belobigen	laud ◇ praise, commend
benachrichtigen	news ◇ inform
beraten	advise/advice ◇ advise, counsel; deliberate; consult with
beratschlagen	piece of advice ◇ deliberate; consult with
bewillkommnen	welcome ◇ welcome [a person], greet

3.2 Iterated Action

beballern	to fire, shoot at ◇ fire at with
befeuern	to fire, shoot at ◇ fire at with
beflicken	to sew ◇ mend clothes repeatedly for
befliegen	to fly ◇ fly on, service [a route]
befragen	to ask ◇ question, consult; interrogate
befragen, sich	ask ◇ consult with [e.g. experts] on
befüllen	to fill [theme] into [location], fill [location] with [theme] ◇ fill [location] with [theme] repeatedly
behämmern	hammer* ◇ work [on location] with [hammer]
beheizen	to heat [e.g. room]; fire [stove]; use [type of fuel] ◇ heat [e.g. house, public swimming pool]
behindern	to stop from ◇ get in the way; obstruct; hinder, impede; handicap [person]
belüften	to air [room] ◇ ventilate [e.g. computer, aquarium]
benummern	number ◇ put serial numbers on, number
beschießen	to shoot at ◇ put under fire
beschmeissen	throw [theme] at [location] ◇ pelt with
betanken	to fill up [location] with [theme] ◇ tank up, refuel [location] with [theme]
bewerfen	throw [theme] at [location] ◇ pelt with

bewettern	weather ◇ ventilate [mine shaft]
beziehen	to pull ◇ subscribe to [e.g. newspaper]; get [supplies] delivered from; be paid [salary] by
beziffern	number ◇ number

3.3 Intensive Action/State

befürchten	to be afraid, fear ◇ suspect, expect
beherrschen	to rule over ◇ dominate, control
bekämpfen	to fight against ◇ fight, combat
belehren	to teach ◇ instruct, inform
benagen	nibble at◇chew up, gnaw
berennen	to run against ◇ storm, attack
berücken	to move, shift ◇ enchant, bewitch
berühren	to touch ◇ concern, stir
beschimpfen	to scold◇verbally abuse
beschwören	to swear, conjure ◇ implore
besiegen	to be victorious over, be the winner ◇ defeat
bestrafen	to punish ◇ sentence, punish
bestürmen	to storm ◇ storm; implore
betreffen	to hit; meet; impact ◇ concern
bewirtschaften	economy, household/to keep house, run an economy ◇ cultivate, work [a farm]

3.4 Affecting

bebacken	to bake ◇ bake for
bedecken	to cover ◇ have sexual intercourse (among horses)
beduseln, sich	dopey ◇ get intoxicated with alcohol
beflammen	flame* ◇ to flame [an internet user]
beflunkern	to lie ◇ lie to
begatten	mate ◇ have sexual intercourse (among mammals)
begleichen	equal [adj.]/equal, resemble ◇ settle [a bill]
behacken	trim by chopping
behauen	hew ◇ shape with blows of axe, hammer
bekehren	to turn ◇ convert [to a faith]

bekiffen, sich	to smoke pot ◇ get intoxicated with pot
beknien	to kneel ◇ beg (on one's knees) to do
bekochen	to cook◇ cook for
bekümmern	to worry ◇ make worried
belabern	to blather ◇ annoy with one's blather
belasten	load*, weight/weigh ◇ stress; weight
belästigen	burdensome ◇ molest
belegen	to lay ◇ have sexual intercourse (among horses, cattle, dogs)
belügen	to lie ◇ lie to
bemogeln	to swindle, be dishonest ◇ swindle somebody
benebeln	fog ◇ befuddle, make dopey
benennen	to name ◇ give a name, label
bequasseln	to blather ◇ annoy with one's blather
bequatschen	to blather ◇ annoy with one's blather
besaufen, sich	to drink, guzzle ◇ get intoxicated with alcohol
beschädigen	to damage, hurt ◇ damage
beschämen	to be ashamed ◇ put to shame, embarrass
bescheissen	shit* ◇ cheat
beschlafen	to sleep ◇ have sexual intercourse (among humans)
beschlagen	to hit ◇ have sexual intercourse (among deer)
beschummeln	to swindle, be dishonest ◇ swindle somebody
beschuppen	scale ◇ cheat, swindle
beschwafeln	to blather ◇ annoy with one's blather
beschwindeln	to swindle, be dishonest ◇ swindle somebody
besprechen	to speak ◇ heal, cure by speaking to
bespringen	to jump ◇ have sexual intercourse (among goats)
bestäuben	dust ◇ pollinate
bestechen	to prick, sting ◇ bribe
besteuern	tax ◇ tax with [tax]; tax at [rate]

bestricken	to knit ◇ do knitting for
bestürzen	to fall, tumble ◇ startle, confound
betanzen	to dance ◇ affect with one's dancing
beteiligen	part ◇ give a part of, a stake in
betrinken, sich	to drink ◇ get intoxicated with alcohol
betrügen	be misleading, be deceptive ◇ cheat
beweihräuchern	incense ◇ adulate, eulogize
bewerben	to woo ◇ advertise [product, market]
bezechen, sich	to booze ◇ get intoxicated with alcohol
bezeichnen	to make a mark on ◇ mark with; call [a person] [a name, label]

3.5 Acting in a Particular Capacity

becircen	Circe ◇ bewitch
befeinden	enemy ◇ act hostile to
befreunden, sich	friend ◇ become friends with
begaunern	crook ◇ con
behexen	witch ◇ bewitch
bemuttern	mother ◇ mother, nanny
bespitzeln	spy ◇ spy on
bevatern	father ◇ behave as a father toward
bevormunden	legal guardian ◇ treat like a child, patronize
bewirten	host ◇ host
bezeugen	witness ◇ testify to; vouch for

4 Surrounding and Containment

bebinden	to bind ◇ bind with
beerdigen	earth ◇ bury
befassen, sich	contain, hold ◇ concern oneself with, deal with
beflechten	to weave, bind ◇ weave with
begreifen	to grasp ◇ understand
begrenzen	border* ◇ form the border of, demarcate; limit
begrenzen	border* ◇ mark off; limit, restrict [location] with [theme]
behausen	house ◇ house
beheimaten	home ◇ house, be home to

beherbergen	shelter, hostel ◇ put up, accommodate; contain, hold
beinhalten	contents ◇ contain
beklemmen	to squeeze, wedge, jam ◇ make uneasy, oppress
belagern	to camp ◇ beleaguer
bemänteln	coat ◇ cloak, disguise, cover up
beranken	to curl around ◇ curl all over
beschleichen	to sneak, prowl ◇ creep over
beschränken	barrier ◇ restrict; curb
bespülen	wash up, rinse ◇ wash up against
bestricken	rope ◇ charm, bewitch, entangle
bewickeln	to wrap around ◇ wrap with, in

5 Removal

beangeln	to fish ◇ fish [body of water]
beerben	to inherit ◇ inherit [source]
befeilen	to file ◇ file [location] smooth
befischen	to fish ◇ fish [body of water]
beheben	lift ◇ repair [damage]; remedy [state of affairs]
behobeln	plane* ◇ plane [location] smooth, plane in shape
bejagen	hunt ◇ hunt in [a territory]
beholzen	wood ◇ clear-cut [forest]
beklauen	steal [theme] from [location] ◇ rob [source]
bemausen	mouse ◇ rob [source]
bemopsen	to steal [theme] from [source]◇ rob [source]
berauben	to steal theme from [source] ◇ rob, deprive [source]
beräumen	clear away; clear [location] of [theme] ◇ clear [location]
bestehlen	to steal [theme] from [source] ◇ rob [source]

6 Proximity

behalten	to hold ◇ keep
beharren	to wait ◇ not move; insist on
bekommen	come ◇ obtain, get
belangen	reach ◇ sue, prosecute
belassen	to leave, let ◇ leave [theme] at [location]
beruhen	to rest ◇ rest on; be based on, founded on
beseitigen	side ◇ eliminate
bestehen	to stand ◇ be in existence; insist on; pass [exam, challenge]
besteigen	to go up ◇ mount, climb, enter
betreten	to step, tread ◇ enter

7 Pseudo-Applicative Participles

beamtet	office ◇ being state appointed, holding state office
bedeppert	idiot ◇ dumb
befangen	catch ◇ biassed; inhibited, shy
befiedert	feather ◇ feathered
beflissen	assiduous, keen
behaart	hair ◇ hairy
beherzt	heart ◇ courageous, brave
bekloppt	to knock ◇ stupid
beknackt	to crack ◇ crazy, nuts
beleibt	body ◇ stout, portly
belemmert	sheep ◇ stupid
beleumundet	held in [good, bad] repute
bemittelt	means ◇ rich
bemoost	moss ◇ old, used in the expression *bemoostes Haupt* 'old man' lit. mossy head
bemützt	cap ◇ wearing a cap
benachbart	neighbor ◇ neighboring, close by; related [e.g. topic]
bepelzt	fur ◇ furry
bereift	hoarfrost ◇ covered with hoarfrost, frost-covered
beritten	ride ◇ mounted, on horseback

berühmt	fame ◇ famous
beschrankt	barrier, gate ◇ having a barrier
beschuht	shoe ◇ wearing shoes
beschürzt	apron ◇ wearing an apron
bestiefelt	boots ◇ wearing boots
bestrumpft	socks ◇ wearing socks
betagt	day ◇ old
betucht	cloth ◇ well-heeled
bewaldet	forest ◇ wooded
beweibt	woman ◇ hitched up with a woman
bewimpert	eyelash ◇ having eyelashes

8 Verbs and Participles that Could not be Assigned to any Class

bedingen	cause, give rise to; require, call for
befehlen	to order, command
befehligen	to be in charge of [troops]
befugen	to authorize, give permission [to do]
begegnen	to encounter
begehren	desire, crave for
beginnen	begin, start
begleiten	to accompany
behaupten	head ◇ maintain, claim
behelligen	to bother, trouble
bekleiden	dress* ◇ hold [office]
bekommen	to come ◇ get, receive
belaufen	to run ◇ amount to
bemüßigt	idle ◇ having the liberty, freedom [to do]; duty-bound, obliged [to do]
benehmen, sich	to take ◇ behave, conduct oneself
benutzen	to make use of ◇ use, employ
beordern	order* ◇ order (to go) to
berechnen	to do sums, calculate, make a calculation ◇ calculate, figure out [e.g. a price]
berichten	to right, correct, straight ◇ report
besagen	to say ◇ mean
beschaffen	to create ◇ provide
bescheiden	to leave; separate ◇ notify, advise

bescheren	to give [location, recipient] [theme]
bescheuert	nuts, crazy
beschickert	tiddly, slightly drunk
beschließen	to shut ◇ determine, decide
beschreiten	to step ◇ tread [a path]
beschwichtigen	to appease, calm down
beschwören	to swear ◇ conjure up
bespiegeln	mirror* ◇ depict, mirror
bestallen	to appoint to
bestatten	place ◇ bury
besteigen	to climb ◇ climb onto
bestimmen	voice ◇ determine
besuchen	seek ◇ visit
beteuern	dear ◇ swear to, vow
betonen	tone ◇ stress, emphasize
betragen	to carry ◇ amount to
betragen, sich	to carry ◇ behave
betrauen	to entrust with
betreiben	to drive ◇ pursue, take part in; carry out; run
betreten	step ◇ enter
betüteln, sich	get intoxicated with alcohol
betütern, sich	get intoxicated with alcohol
bewähren, sich	to last ◇ prove oneself, prove one's worth
bewahrheiten, sich	truth ◇ prove to be true
bewältigen	to cope with, manage
bewegen	way ◇ move
beweisen	to point to, direct at ◇ prove
bewenden	only in the idiom *es bei etwas bewenden lassen* 'leave it at something, not pursue further than'
bewerben,sich	to woo ◇ apply for
bewerkstelligen	to bring about, manage that
bewilligen	will ◇ allow, agree to
bewirken	to work; function ◇ cause, bring about
bezahlen	to pay [for a good; a person] ◇ [for a good; a person]
bezeigen	to show ◇ show, express [emotion]; grant [favor]

bezichtigen	to accuse of
bleiben	to remain

References

Alsina, Alex and Sam Mchombo. 1990. The Syntax of Applicatives in Chichewa: Problems for a Theta Theoretic Asymmetry. *Natural Language and Linguistic Theory* 8:493–506.

Bennet, Michael and Barbara Partee. 1978. *Toward the Logic of Tense and Aspect in English.* Indianapolis: Indiana University Linguistics Club.

Bickel, Balthasar. 1997. Aspectual Scope and the Difference between Logical and Semantic Representation. *Lingua* 102:115–131.

Bierwisch, Manfred. 1988. On the Grammar of Local Prepositions. In M. B. et al., ed., *Syntax, Semantik und Lexikon*, pages 1–65. Berlin: Akademie-Verlag.

Bresnan, Joan. 1994. Locative Inversion and the Architecture of Universal Grammar. *Language* 70:72–131.

Brinkmann, Ursula. 1997. *The Locative Alternation in German: Its Structure and Acquisition.* Amsterdam: John Benjamins.

Bybee, Joan. 1985. *Morphology: A Study in the Relationship between Meaning and Form.* Philadelphia: Benjamins.

Bybee, Joan. 1995. Regular Morphology and the Lexicon. *Language and Cognitive Processes* 10:425–455.

Clark, Eve and Herbert Clark. 1979. When Nouns Surface as Verbs. *Language* 55:767–811.

Dowty, David. 1991. Thematic Proto-roles and Argument Selection. *Language* 67:547–619.

Eroms, Hans-Werner. 1980. *Be-Verb und Präpositionalphrase.* Heidelberg: Carl Winter Universitätsverlag.

Fauconnier, Gilles. 1985. *Mental Spaces.* Chicago: University of Chicago Press.

Fauconnier, Gilles and Mark Turner. 1996. Blending as a Central Process of Grammar. In A. Goldberg, ed., *Conceptual Structure, Discourse and Language*, pages 113–130. Stanford: CSLI Publications.

Filip, Hana. 1994. Aspect and the Semantics of Noun Phrases. In C. Vetters, ed., *Tense and Aspect in Discourse*, pages 227–255. Berlin: Mouton de Gruyter.

Fillmore, Charles J. 1977. The Case for Case Reopened. In P. Cole and J. M. Sadock, eds., *Grammatical Relations*, vol. 8 of *Syntax and Semantics*, pages 3–26. New York: Academic Press.

Fillmore, Charles J. 1982. Frame Semantics. In L. S. of Korea, ed., *Linguistics in the Morning Calm*, pages 111–38. Seoul: Hanshin.

Fillmore, Charles J. 1985. Frames and the Semantics of Understanding. *Quaderni di Semantica* 6(2):222–253.

Fillmore, Charles J. 1986. Pragmatically Controlled Zero Anaphora. *Berkeley Linguistics Society* 12:95–107.

Fillmore, Charles J. and Paul Kay. 1997. Construction Grammar. Manuscript, University of California, Berkeley.

Foley, William and Robert Van Valin. 1984. *Functional Syntax and Universal Grammar*. Cambridge: Cambridge University Press.

Göbel, Ulrich and Oskar Reichmann, eds. 1999. *Frühneuhochdeutsches Wörterbuch*. Berlin: Walter de Gruyter.

Goldberg, Adele. 1995. *Constructions: A Construction Grammar Approach to Argument Structure*. Chicago: University of Chicago Press.

Goldberg, Adele. 1997. The Relationships between Verbs and Constructions. In R. Dirven and E. Sweetser, eds., *Lexical and Syntactical Constructions and the Construction of Meaning*, pages 383–398. Amsterdam: Benjamins.

Gropen, Jess, Steven Pinker, Michelle Hollander, and Richard Goldberg. 1991. Affectedness and Direct Objects: The Role of Lexical Semantics in the Acquisition of Argument Structure. *Cognition* 41:153–195.

Gropen, Jess, Steven Pinker, Michelle Hollander, Richard Goldberg, and Ronald Wilson. 1989. The Learnability and Acquisition of the Dative Alternation in English. *Language* 65:203–257.

Herweg, Michael. 1991. A Critical Account of two Classical Approaches to Aspect. *Journal of Semantics* 8:362–403.

Hinkelman, Elizabeth A. and James F. Allen. 1989. Two Constraints on Speech Act Ambiguity. In *Proceedings of the Twenty-seventh Annual Meeting of the Association for Computational Linguistics*.

Hopper, Paul J. 1985. Causes and Affects. *Chicago Linguistic Society* 21(2):67–88.

Hopper, Paul J. and Sandra A. Thompson. 1980. Transitivity in Grammar and Discourse. *Language* 56:251–299.

Hopper, Paul J. and Elizabeth C. Traugott. 1993. *Grammaticalization*. Cambridge: Cambridge University Press.

Horn, Lawrence. 1989. *A Natural History of Negation*. Chicago: Chicago University Press.

Jackendoff, Ray. 1983. *Semantics and Cognition*. Cambridge, MA: MIT Press.

Jackendoff, Ray. 1990. *Semantic Structures*. Cambridge, MA: MIT Press.

Jackendoff, Ray. 1997a. *The Architecture of the Language Faculty*. Cambridge, MA: MIT Press.

Jackendoff, Ray. 1997b. Twistin' the Night Away. *Language* 73:534–570.

Kay, Paul and Charles J. Fillmore. 1999. Grammatical Constructions and Linguistic Generalizations: The What's X Doing Y? Construction. *Language* 75:1–33.

König, Ekkehard and Elizabeth Traugott. 1988. Pragmatic Strengthening and Semantic Change: The Conventionalizing of Conversational Implicature. In W. Hullen and R. Schulze, eds., *Understanding the Lexicon: Meaning, Sense and World Knowledge in Lexical Semantics*, pages 110–124. Tübingen: Niemeyer.

Lakoff, George. 1987. *Women, Fire, and Dangerous Things: What Categories Reveal about the Human Mind*. Chicago: University of Chicago Press.

Lakoff, George. 1990. The Invariance Hypothesis: Is Abstract Reason Based on Image-Schemas? *Cognitive Linguistics* 1:39–74.

Lakoff, George and Mark Johnson. 1980. *Metaphors we Live by*. Chicago: University of Chicago Press.

Langacker, Ronald W. 1987. *Foundations of Cognitive Grammar*, vol. I: Theoretical Prerequisites. Stanford: Stanford University Press.

Langacker, Ronald W. 1991. *Foundations of Cognitive Grammar*, vol. II: Descriptive Application. Stanford, CA: Stanford University Press.

Lebeaux, David. 1988. The Feature [+affected] and the Formation of the Passive. In W. Wilkins, ed., *Thematic Relations*, vol. 21 of *Syntax and Semantics*, pages 243–262. New York: Academic Press.

Levin, Beth. 1993. *English Verb Classes and Alternations: A Preliminary Investigation*. Chicago: University of Chicago Press.

Lexer, Matthias. 1872. *Mittelhochdeutsches Handwörterbuch*. Leipzig: Verlag von S. Hirzel.

Löbner, Sebastian. 1990. *Wahr neben falsch: Duale Operatoren als die Quantoren natürlicher Sprache*. Tübingen, Germany: Niemeyer.

Losiewicz, Beth. 1992. *The Effect of Frequency on Linguistic Morphology*. Doctoral, University of Texas at Austin, Austin.

Marcus, Gary F., Ursula Brinkmann, Harald Clahsen, Richard Wiese, and Steven Pinker. 1995. German Inflection: The Exception that Proves the Rule. *Cognitive Psychology* 29:189–256.

Michaelis, Laura A. 1993. On Deviant Case-marking in Latin. In R. D. Van Valin, ed., *Advances in Role and Reference Grammar*, pages 311–373. Amsterdam: Benjamins.

Michaelis, Laura A. and Knud Lambrecht. 1996. Toward a Construction-Based Model of Language Use: The Case of Nominal Extraposition. *Language* 72:215–247.

Morgan, Jerry. 1978. Two Types of Convention in Indirect Speech Acts. In P. Cole, ed., *Pragmatics*, vol. 9 of *Syntax and Semantics*, pages 261–280. New York: Academic Press.

Pinker, Steven. 1989. *Learnability and Cognition: The Acquisition of Argument Structure*. Cambridge, MA: MIT Press.

Pinker, Steven and Alan Prince. 1991. Regular and Irregular Morphology and the Psychological Status of Rules of Grammar. *Berkeley Linguistics Society* 17:230–251.

Rappaport, Malka and Beth Levin. 1988. What to do with Theta Roles. In W. Wilkins, ed., *Thematic Relations*, vol. 21 of *Syntax and Semantics*, pages 7–36. New York: Academic Press.

Reddy, Michael. 1979. The Conduit Metaphor. In A. Ortony, ed., *Metaphor and Thought*. Cambridge: Cambridge University Press.

Regier, Terry. 1994. A Preliminary Study of the Semantics of Reduplication. Techreport TR-94-019, International Computer Science Institute, Berkeley, CA.

Ruppenhofer, Josef. 1999. Lexical Change across a Semantic Class. Paper presented at the annual meeting of the Linguistic Society of America, Los Angeles.

Slobin, Dan. 1997. There's More than One Way to Talk about Motion: Consequences of Linguistic Typology for Narrative Style. Paper presented at the Third Conference on Conceptual Structure, Discourse and Language, University of Colorado at Boulder.

Sweetser, Eve. 1990. *From Etymology to Pragmatics*. Cambridge: Cambridge University Press.

Talmy, Leonard. 1985. Lexicalization Patterns: Semantic Structure in Lexical Forms. In T. Shopen, ed., *Grammatical Categories and the Lexicon*, vol. 3 of *Language Typology and Syntactic Description*, pages 57–149. Cambridge: Cambridge University Press.

Talmy, Leonard. 1988. The Relation of Grammar to Cognition. In B. Rudzka-Östyn, ed., *Topics in Cognitive Linguistics*, pages 57–149. Amsterdam: Benjamins.

Tenny, Carol. 1987. *Grammaticalizing Aspect and Affectedness*. doctoral, MIT, Cambridge, MA.

Van Valin, Robert D. and Randy J. Lapolla. 1997. *Syntax: Structure, Meaning and Function*. Cambridge: Cambridge University Press.

Wunderlich, Dieter. 1987. An Investigation of Lexical Composition: The Case of German *be-* verbs. *Linguistics* 25:283–331.

Wunderlich, Dieter. 1991. How do Prepositional Phrases Fit into Compositional Syntax and Semantics? *Linguistics* 29:591–621.

Wunderlich, Dieter. 1992. Cause and the Structure of Verbs. Arbeiten des SFB *Theorie des Lexikons*, Heinrich-Heine-Universität Düsseldorf.

Wunderlich, Dieter. 1994. Towards a Lexicon-based Theory of Agreement. *Theoretical Linguistics* 20:1–35.

Wunderlich, Dieter. 1997. Cause and the Structure of Verbs. *Linguistic Inquiry* 28:27–68.

Zwicky, Arnold. 1989. What's become of Derivations? Defaults and Invocation. *Berkeley Linguistics Society* 15:303–320.

Zwicky, Arnold. 1994. Dealing out Meaning: Fundamentals of Syntactic Constructions. *Berkeley Linguistics Society* 20:611–625.

Index